BEING OF TWO MINDS

Being of Two Minds

MODERNIST LITERARY CRITICISM
AND EARLY MODERN TEXTS

Jonathan Goldberg

FORDHAM UNIVERSITY PRESS   NEW YORK 2022

Fordham University Press has no responsibility for the
persistence or accuracy of URLs for external or third-
party Internet websites referred to in this publication and
does not guarantee that any content on such websites is,
or will remain, accurate or appropriate.

Fordham University Press also publishes its books in a
variety of electronic formats. Some content that appears
in print may not be available in electronic books.

Visit us online at www.fordhampress.com.

Library of Congress Cataloging-in-Publication Data
available online at https://catalog.loc.gov.

Printed in the United States of America

24 23 22   5 4 3 2 1

First edition

Contents

BEING OF TWO MINDS

Introduction

Being of Two Minds explores literary critical thinking. The literary criticism of T. S. Eliot, Virginia Woolf, and William Empson are the sites for this exploration; a chapter is devoted to each of them and their pursuit of questions about the nature of their practice. These questions arise from the ontology of texts, a complex territory, since ontological questions occur in multiple registers. There is, perhaps first, the question of the kind of reality one enters in the act of reading and interpreting a text. There follow the questions texts pose as their subject — ultimate concerns: questions about life and death, individuality and relationality, among others. Such questions came to seem especially fraught in the early years of the twentieth century as old assurances about artistic forms as well as ways of organizing meaningful lives appeared to have frayed irreparably. Willa Cather's pronouncement in the preface to her collection of literary critical essays, *Not Above Forty*, that "the world broke in two in 1922 or thereabouts," echoes similar statements by Virginia Woolf, who declared that "on or about December 1910 human character changed" in perhaps her best-known work of literary criticism, *Mr. Bennett and Mrs. Brown.*[1] A few years later she wondered, in *A Room of One's Own*, if the First World War marked that watershed in human consciousness. The exact date is not the question so much as the dilemmas raised by this supposed break: how to live; how to write. The two questions are entwined in the thinking of the three authors I consider in this book — not that they arrive at the same answers to these questions; not, in fact, that answers are what they (or I) seek to deliver. The shared point about the thinking exemplified in the writing I examine is that it does not come to an end so long as one is able to go on thinking; indeed, at moments, each of the three entertain the possibility that thought goes on even when the individual can think no longer. This thought can arise from realizing that the reading of a text is never fully finished. We know that from the obvious fact that readings are answered by other readings, our own as well as those made by other critics, whether they further an interpretation, complicate it, dispute it; no reading ever delivers a final definitive meaning. The dilemma that modernists felt had come to a crisis has not been solved, nor can it be; the issues raised then remain.

The scope of issues is vast, as even this brief preliminary sketch suggests; this book and the body of work it considers do not to seek to answer them, certainly do not suppose there is an answer to them. I try to stay close to the texts at hand while recognizing that the ontological questions raised trespass the border between the literary and the philosophical (and perhaps the religious, as well). A particular focus of the period guides and limits me. It's the one T. S. Eliot announced in "The Metaphysical Poets," a 1921 essay that represents a moment in Eliot's thinking that he quickly came to repudiate and that, nonetheless, caught hold. (It was F. R.

Leavis and the contributors to *Scrutiny* that first continued to promote Eliot's radical revisions to the canon.)[2] Eliot had declared in the face of a dilemma felt by many of his compeers — the task that Ezra Pound memorably enunciated in the phrase "make it new" — that metaphysical poetry offered a model of how to proceed — how to make the past new as much as how to introduce something new when the old seemed no longer meaningful. The metaphysicals, to Eliot, showed the way: following them "the poet must become more and more comprehensive, more allusive, more indirect, in order to force, to dislocate, if necessary, language into his meaning."[3]

These qualities, this violence, which had led Dr. Johnson to regard the metaphysicals as outliers, were for Eliot, at this point, guides to "the direct current of English poetry" as it once had been and might yet be practiced again in order to tackle genuine poetic questions. Eliot parsed these as the relationship between thought and feeling. Its current sundering had begun with Milton and Dryden; one could instead look to Donne (perhaps paramount among others) not just to get back the soul that Milton had divorced from body in poetry, but "the cerebral cortex, the nervous system, and the digestive tract," as well (290).

Eliot's 1921 call is in line with his thinking in "Tradition and the Individual Talent," his 1919 brief for a new poetry that would answer tradition at the same time as it rewrote it. One way that would happen was by finding figures like Donne, once marginalized, as rather contributory to the "direct current" and thus able to stand by Homer, Greek tragedy, Dante, and Shakespeare without unseating them but nonetheless allowing "the really new" (15) to reorganize a past made present, a past no longer past. Eliot suggested that it would not be "preposterous" that the new could reorder the old, even as he also proposed that "the most individual parts" of the work of the modern poet "may be those in which the dead poets, his ancestors, assert themselves most vigorously" (14). This book starts with a close reading of Eliot's "Tradition and the Individual Talent" not only for its importance as a manifesto for modernist literary theory and practice, but because formulations like these, in which the past seems never to die and yet to require a resuscitation by the present, press hard on ordinary logics and categorical distinctions of before and after, opening paths to nondualistic thinking, a condition of being of two minds at once that, in this instance, raises questions about temporality. In question is the temporality of life and of textual life; such questions are raised by each of the critics I read in this book, but not in the same way.

Eliot presses metaphor to do what one might expect a more propositional writing to convey. Although he often writes as if he were presenting a logically sequential case, it falls apart the closer one looks. I explore these gaps — especially those that announce themselves as such. I do not pursue a hermeneutics of suspicion, a desire to reveal some hidden truth. Rather, I follow Giorgio Agamben, who, asking, "What Is the Act of Creation," takes joy in those moments when a text reveals "its capacity to be developed," often by what it leaves unspoken. If we enter the discussion there, "we inevitably end up at a point where it is not possible to distinguish between what is ours and what belongs to the author we are reading." Agamben calls this place a "zone of indifference" that he ties to the notion of potentiality in Aristotle.[4] The sole literary quotation in "Tradition and the Individual Talent" comes from an early modern text, *The Revenger's Tragedy*, conspicuously unidentified by Eliot. At the end of the essay another unidentified text is cited, this time quoted in Greek; it comes from *De Anima* 1.4, 408b, a speculative sentence about mind (*nous*) being eternal in which Aristotle wonders if our own minds might have access to an eternal mind.[5] How can we, who live in mortal bodies, also exist beyond our mortal selves? Eliot halts and holds at this borderline state. He remains a being of two minds, bound to the life of the body, bound to the life of the mind. Midway in his essay, Eliot suggests that a metaphor may explain how the poet enters the condition of impersonality requisite for the poetic existence that represents the poet's relation to the past as well as to present readers a state of mind perhaps akin to Agamben's "indifference." Eliot's essay continually crosses between the positions of the poet and the reader in its attempt to establish where the poem takes place. His metaphor of a catalytic conversion results in a change in elements to produce a sulfuric mixture that yet leaves a thread of platinum unchanged, a strange passage that I follow through Eliot's allusion to Dante meeting his teacher Brunetto Latini in the sulfuric circle of sodomites as a plot for his redescription of literary history. Sexual recastings also can be glimpsed in the projects of Woolf and Empson, although not in Eliot's terms. Indeed, that is a central point in this book: that these modernist writers may share a critical project but that each is framed differently, in terminology, in the literary examples chosen to examine. Those differences reflect different ways of thinking, including differences in the responses of Woolf and Empson to aspects of Eliot's thinking.

Woolf can be supposed in dialogue with Eliot in *A Room of One's Own* and the two volumes of *The Common Reader*, although that is not something she makes explicit in her rethinking of the canon under the pressure of the present moment.[6] Eliot's canon is male territory. In *A Room of One's Own*, the text I first explore, Woolf questions the absence of a tradition of women writers, turning over the question from a number of angles. Can that absence simply be assumed, she asks, given that the history of women, even the definition of what a woman is, has been delivered almost entirely by men whose gender seems to be what qualifies them to provide what passes for fact and truth? These facts are nothing but motivated fictions; Woolf answers in kind, and in both registers: she provides a roll call of earlier women writers (in it, Aphra Behn is the first woman to have earned a living from her writing, a woman whose sexuality does not seem to have been ordered by patriarchal prescriptions); she creates a fictional woman writer whose existence may perhaps be believed. Woolf names that woman Judith Shakespeare, twin sister to her brother Will, identical to him in every respect except gender (in that respect like the twins Viola and Sebastian in *Twelfth Night*). Her imagining a female Shakespeare resonates with Eliot's call to look back to the early seventeenth century for predecessors to current poetic practice.

Being of two minds, Woolf insists on both the possibility that such a woman might have existed and the likelihood that she didn't. Her solution to this seemingly impossible coincident ontological duality lies in the likelihood that the Anonymous who so often appears in early modern collections of verse might well name a woman writer. The naming of the woman without a name might seem very far away from the name "Shakespeare" until one realizes, as Woolf insists, that his proper name names his canonical status, not the person. When we say "Shakespeare," it is not the man we mean so much as the writer of his texts, the man who gets a name from his work. "Shakespeare" names him as canonical. Anon, too, may name the nameless woman writer who exists in her writing. The author of *A Room of One's Own* presents herself as nameless. Woolf answers Eliot in his own terms and by reversing them. Her anonymous and his impersonal share negations (a-, im-) that attach them to their supposed opposites, the name and the person. Even these terms can be turned around: persons, etymologically speaking, are masks. The proper name, as Shakespeare's punning sonnets on "will" insist, is hardly univocal or only self-referential. Both he and his beloved have wills.

Woolf thus twins ontological questions about the reality of fictions and the reality of personal existence. They come together on the last page of A Room of One's Own when she expresses her "belief . . . that the poet who never wrote a word and was buried at the crossroads still lives. Judith Shakespeare lives," Woolf continues, "in you and me" precisely because "great poets do not die; they are continuing presences."[7] The life of the poet is not the same as mortal life, yet it also coincides with our life, the life that we, "you and me," addressed in these words, confer. These readers include others than the person reading those words at any moment, and some who read are as undoubtedly dead as the author who wrote them. The life in the text is not simply there. Woolf designates the life she has in mind as "the common life which is the real life and not . . . the little separate lives we live as individuals." That, Woolf continues, is the world she would have us realize that we inhabit "and not only the world of men and women." We are enjoined to recognize that we live in two worlds at once, the one we ordinarily inhabit and assume to be the world and the one Woolf calls "reality," a world lived in common and beyond not only the demarcations that separate "you and me" but that join us in a life not our own, nor one bounded by the parameter of mortality. It is not an afterlife but rather the life that continues after us, in other people, and in the world we leave when we die but that continues without us. That continuing world includes the ones poets imagine and put into words. It is true, as Gertrude tells Hamlet, that we all have death in common, but it also is true that we each die

our own death but can all participate in the imaginative life
that texts offer.

That common life is one of the meanings of "common"
in Woolf's project of *The Common Reader*, sets of essays,
most of them previously published in venues like *TLS*, gathered, selected, edited, but also including essays written to
fill out its project to cover a range of English literature (and
a few examples from other national literatures) that extends
far beyond the all-male canon Eliot imagines to constitute
"the mind of Europe." Woolf includes works by women,
many of them written in forms that would not immediately
be categorized as literature; she focuses often on the representations of women in the works she considers or pairs canonical and noncanonical authors as she does in an essay on
Chaucer and the Paston letters. My discussion of *The Common Reader* looks closely at that essay among the additional
ones Woolf provided to supplement the ones she chose.
They are often essays on early literature: Eliot had called
for a widening of the canon beyond those already included;
Woolf adds women writers, women patrons, women readers,
women characters, exceeding and abrading Eliot's agenda
for literature. Woolf writes about the Greeks not as forebears,
but to distinguish them from us; she probes the question of
whether we can understand these texts — we can't, and that's
why we keep returning to them. They are not assimilable to
a singular vision of the West that runs uninterrupted from
the classics to the present. Their world is anything but the
one Christianity misshaped.

Woolf's procedures in these essays involve continually
rethinking and reframing. Jacobean drama widens our
imaginations and clogs them; its characters are not so much
lifelike as life forces, violences, Woolf calls them. The
language in early modern texts is too rhetorical to deliver
immediately recognizable people, but nonetheless does at

stunning moments. Woolf's approach is epitomized in her treatment of Montaigne, the one early modern non-English figure she treats. He displaces the expected Shakespeare, a writer Woolf read over and again, as unpublished notes reveal and her diary records, but who barely gets a mention in *The Common Reader*. Montaigne's motto, *"Que sçais-je,"* might well be Woolf's. She rethinks everything she writes, as does he, not erasing first thoughts but letting second thoughts stand beside them, however much they may be contradictory. In following her thought (his thought) we are offered a model of thinking and of self-conscious existence in which part of the joy of being alive is the elation of thinking beyond what one might have thought. Woolf weighs over and again the congruence and disparities between early texts and current ones.

Woolf has other terms for this way of being; in *A Room of One's Own*, it is androgyny. The book starts by reclaiming and rethinking the nature of women, but close to the end decides that its opening sentence should not have been one about women and literature but rather "that it is fatal for any one who writes to think of their sex. It is fatal to be a man or a woman pure and simple; one must be women-manly or man-womanly" (102–3).[8] Woolf is not denying that one is a man or a woman; her "must be" is based in a conviction about the mind, that it has no singular gender, and how that makes for great writing. "A great mind is androgynous"; Shakespeare is "the type of the androgynous" (97). This crossing of gender is not incompatible with Woolf's advocacy of a modern novel that might feature the same-sex couple Chloe and Olivia, for it roots same-sex desire in cross-gender identification. This is a quite different way of linking the reality of another mode of being to literature than Eliot's male-male literary history; its welcome sodomitical genealogical plot can be taken as the more usual homosocial one.[9]

The question of how we as readers are attached to what we read is radicalized in Woolf's late, incomplete autobiographical "A Sketch of the Past," at which I glance at the conclusion of my chapter on her. She discusses there what she terms "moments of Being," jolting flashes that take her from the ordinary nonbeing of a routinized life to the reality she affirms at the conclusion of A *Room of One's Own* and experiences in her life and her work as a writer of fiction. Readers find in artistic creation the other life of that experience; in it, we know that "there is no Shakespeare, there is no Beethoven; certainly and emphatically there is no God; we are the words; we are the music; we are the thing itself."[10] Woolf approaches here something like the Heideggerian understanding that Being is what beings (*Dasein*) apprehend and make palpable in creative acts that take us out of ourselves, in one sense, and into what we are, in another. The experience of being of two minds is not transcendentalizing, but more like the sensing of potentiality that Agamben finds in passages on mind like the one Eliot quoted from *De anima* at the end of "Tradition and the Individual Talent."

At the opening of his contribution to a 1948 volume honoring T. S. Eliot, William Empson makes this striking confession to explain why he will not be judging or defining Eliot's accomplishments: "I do not know for certain how much of my own mind he invented."[11] Empson withholds judgment, it seems, fearing that making claims about Eliot he may be judging himself; the boundaries between their minds are uncertain. Anything he may say about one might be equally true (or false) about the other. Empson treats himself as an aftereffect of Eliot, made, created, through his reading. This space between reader, writer, and text is Empson's interpretive domain. In this formulation he seems entirely passive. Yet, his claim boomerangs: Empson is jus-

tifying withholding the praise that the occasion requires. He
more or less admits this as he continues his sentence. He
does not know how much of his mind Eliot invented, "let
alone how much of it is a reaction against him or indeed a
consequence of misreading him" (361). The effect of reading is not entirely one of acceptance; reaction against what
one reads also is possible. Indeed, "invented," as Empson
well knew, in early modern English could as easily mean
"discovered" as created; in that sense the reaction provoked
by Eliot was the discovery of something in Empson's mind
present before he read Eliot. Empson continues to cover his
tracks: his reading of Eliot, whether in the service of praise
or critique, might well have arisen from misreading; misreading may be impossible to distinguish from reading, a
form of reading, not its opposite. One proof of this Empson
offers immediately when he notes how often anecdotes he
tells about Eliot, meaning to be complimentary, seem to be
received as anything but. Is that because Empson does not
really know what he intends or because any story about Eliot
is bound to be a negative one?

Empson offers a second example of this complex process,
describing first meeting Eliot when he came to deliver the
Clark lectures in Cambridge in 1926, Empson's second year
as a student there. At one of the informal meetings he held
with students, Eliot had claimed never to have read Proust,
but then, at another, he talked for quite some time about
the limitations of the English translation of À la recherche du
temps perdu. Empson absolves Eliot from lying, fairly sure
that what he meant by "reading" was that he had never ventured a reading of Proust, never had written about his novel.
Unless, Empson continues, Eliot wasn't really listening to
the original question and was thus unresponsive rather than
untruthful in his remark about never having read Proust.
The point about this anecdote (it can be extended to others

that Empson tells) is that it reveals something so habitual that
I titled my chapter "Ambiguous Empson." Empson is always
ambiguous, always saying two things at once. The title of his
longest essay in *Some Versions of Pastoral*, "Double Plots,"
could title all his writing. In *Seven Types of Ambiguity*, the
seven types themselves are ambiguous. Any poem Empson
takes up could fit into more than one of them depending on
the angle of approach — for example, on whether he is describing his first encounters with a text or later ones. Poems
don't stand still because minds don't; neither do categories.
Ambiguity is the bottom line. Empson seems to agree with
some early modern mathematicians who claimed (following
Aristotle) that one is no number: a numbering system needs
to be invented as soon as one is willing to include two things
in the same category. "One" is a back formation from "two,"
which is also an adage of deconstructive thought that Empson seems often to be inventing (despite the fact that late
in his career he disavowed any such connection, negating
Derrida as Nerrida).[12]

In the final chapter of *Seven Types of Ambiguity*, Empson offers two contexts for his double takes: one in ancient
languages, or even in early modern versions of English, in
which the same word can bear opposite meanings; "let," in
Shakespeare, can as readily mean what it still does, "allow,
permit," as its opposite: "stop, impede." Hamlet's "let be"
ambiguously welcomes the end, just as "To be or not to be"
opens a soliloquy on the possibility that "or" might mean
"and." Empson summons up Freud's endorsement of a theory of the antithetical sense of primal words and extends
it to a summary sentence about all words: "In so far . . . as
you know that two things are opposites, you know a relation
which connects them."[13] Nothing is without a relationship
to what it supposedly is not. Any noun, once modified, reveals that it is not something by itself, so much so, Empson

claims, that even a noun unmodified will remind us that it needs an adjective to specify it; specification and generalization are tied together. In the preface to the second edition of *Seven Types of Ambiguity*, Empson declared the outrageous premise of his book: that he "would use the term 'ambiguity' to mean whatever [he] liked"; the token of that in the book, Empson told his reader, was "that the distinctions between the Seven Types . . . would not be worth the attention of a profounder thinker" (viii). The profoundest thought will never come to the bottom; to think is always to go on thinking. Arrival is an error or a compromise, something necessary if one is going to make a stab at meaning. Such stabs also can be concessions to received opinions or to conventions that allow one to believe in and sometimes even to achieve communication. In pursuing the course he laid out for himself, Empson recalls telling his supervisor I. A. Richards that he was going to let every mistaken reading fly, imagining that sometime later he would draw distinctions. *Seven Types of Ambiguity* began as an undergraduate thesis and was published when Empson was twenty-four; seventeen years later, preparing a second edition, he found nothing in it to correct. I take that as my warrant only to consider in detail the first two books Empson wrote; the later work follows from where he began.

In the preface to the second edition of *Seven Types of Ambiguity* Empson describes the circumstances of its composition: "At that time Mr. T. S. Eliot's criticism in particular, and the Zeitgeist in general, were calling for a reconsideration of the claims of the nineteenth-century poets so as to get them in perspective with the newly discovered merits of Donne, Marvell, and Dryden" (viii). This statement seems to me a generous misunderstanding of Eliot, who rather suggests the irreparable harm done to poetry by Milton and Dryden that continues to stand in need of repair. Although

Eliot quickly came to reverse himself on Dryden, Milton and the poets of the centuries following remained cautionary examples. Empson heeds Eliot's call insofar as most of his examples are early modern; he claims that the state of the language in that time made it especially productive of ambiguity. However, he does not exclude Milton from brief consideration in *Seven Types of Ambiguity* and devotes a chapter to him in *Some Versions of Pastoral*. By including what Eliot would exclude, Empson's generous misreading becomes generative of his own writing. So, in *Seven Types of Ambiguity* no sooner has he begun on early modern literature than he backtracks to a detailed consideration of Chaucerian ambiguity; Pope is often cited, Shelley's ambiguity defended against Eliot's claims — Swinburne, too. For Empson all poetry that one finds compelling and compelled to understand (the two motives cannot be separated) is ambiguous. While he offers a detailed reading of Donne's "A Valediction: Of Weeping" and of several poems by Herbert, Shakespeare provides Empson with most of his early modern examples. Although Eliot often accorded Shakespeare supreme canonical status, in his only essay exclusively devoted to Shakespeare he faults *Hamlet* for its lack of an objective correlative, its failure to achieve the impersonality of the metaphysicals. For Empson, Shakespeare's ambiguities show him seeking and bending language to account for the most complex states of mind. Shakespeare's sonnets figure at least as often as his plays do, for in them the erotic attachment to an unworthy and yet undeniable beloved allows the poet to endlessly examine the two-sidedness of his implacable thought and feeling. Empson's Shakespeare is entranced by a Mr. W. H. modeled on Oscar Wilde's vision of the beloved. The ambiguity of Shakespeare's love for his master mistress names the eros that drives Empson's reading practices in two directions at once.

That movement can be seen in the 1947 preface; Empson recalls the immediate reception of *Seven Types of Ambiguity* and revisits what he thinks of as its most cogent critical reception, a 1931 review by James Smith. (I use it to frame my discussion of Empson.) Smith poses a central question: whether poetry is a phenomenon, subject to all the contradictions that life offers, and thus of a piece with it, or a noumenon, a piece of life that has been shaped and withdrawn into its own formal and intellectual existence. Empson answers that it is necessarily both. Empson's answer to the quandaries Smith raises in fact mirrors Smith's definition of the metaphysics of metaphysical poetry. "The contradictions in metaphysics . . . spring from essence. The very nature of things brings them forth. It seems impossible that the nature of things should possess either the one or the other of a pair of qualities; it seems impossible that it should possess both together; it seems impossible that it should not possess both."[14] Empson alludes to Smith several times in *Some Versions of Pastoral*, ascribing to him the insoluble philosophical question of the One and the Many — of human relations, of relations between the human and the nonhuman, of the individual and the cosmos, of mortal temporality and life that persists without us, of the life of the mind and the life of the body that are coincident even though the mind posits nonhuman forms of existence, inscribing them in books whose afterlives depend on the readings they receive and solicit. "Is to live in $n+1$ places necessarily more valuable than to live in n?," Empson asks in *Seven Types of Ambiguity*. He enunciates an answer through Proust's discovery "that sometimes when you are living in one place you are reminded of living in another place, and this, since you are living in two places, means that you are outside time, in the only state of beatitude he can imagine." Space doubled becomes time extended beyond its before/after dimensions.

It allows for the refinding of lost past time. Empson avows "such a releasing and knotted duality" as his quarry.[15]

I end my chapter on Empson with his essay on Marvell's "The Garden" in *Some Versions of Pastoral*, exploring Paul de Man's praise of that essay as the best example of Empson's distance from I. A. Richards and from the New Critics. Empson thinks his way from the singular to the general by way of questions of being and thinking, focusing his reading of "The Garden" on its middle stanzas on the mind's capacity to mirror the world but also to annihilate and to recreate it; "either contemplating everything or shutting everything out" is Empson's s initial description of the nature of the mind's activity: "The point is not that these two are essentially different but that they must cease to be different as far as either is to be known."[16] His reading of the poem vibrates from that center to heady formulations like these: "The pastoral figure is always ready to be the critic; he not only includes everything but may in some unexpected way know it" (124); "In including everything in itself the mind includes as a detail itself and all its inclusions"(126); "Though they are essentially unlike they are practically unlike in different degrees at different times; a supreme condition can be imagined, though not attained, in which they are essentially like" (136); "Two ideas are united which in normal use are contradictory, and our machinery of interpretation so acts that we feel there is a series of senses in which they could be more and more truly combined" (139). (This is one of the points when Empson credits James Smith on metaphysical conceits.) Claiming to stay with Marvell, Empson moves to Donne, where "sense" can as easily be a matter of mind or matter, to Shakespeare as desiring and imagining come together in a pun on "feign" and "fain." Writing a poem is not the most direct way to seduce someone; it suggests that something more is at stake than one or the other.

That something more Empson connects, as he opens his essay, to a prompt in Eastern thought he found in Richards; the Western ping-pong of the antinomy of the spiritual and the physical, of freedom and predestination, is displaced by Buddhist explorations in the One and the Many. A fire burns out, but that does not mean the end of fire; a wave crashes on the shore; that does not mean the end of waves. Not being and being coincide, not individually, except in the mind, collectively thinking with and beyond what we read. Empson's approach to literature takes together both/ and, either/or, and neither/nor as the closest one can get to the ever receding, always beckoning prospect of meaning. Any sentence that uses "is" to define one thing as another posits at once sameness and difference.

To reiterate: *Being of Two Minds* aims at the philosophical implications of the processes of literary critical thinking. I do not mean to suggest that Eliot, Woolf, and Empson do this in identical ways, nor does Eliot's call to rethink the possibil- ities for poetry lodged in early modern texts lead Woolf and Empson to the same texts. The way each critic approaches and thinks such questions as how one may be in two places at once or in two times at once, questions about the relations of the One and the Many, self and other, life and death, also necessarily redescribes them. Helen Thaventhiran's *Radical Empiricists: Five Modernist Close Readers* makes a similar argument. Her modernists (Eliot, Richards, Empson, Mar- ianne Moore, and Blackmur) are not identical, a point she demonstrates by identifying unique aspects of each critic's style — Eliot's recourse to citation of favored passages, for ex- ample, or Empson's modeling the possibility of endless am- biguities on the Arden Shakespeare's offer of numerous op- tions textually and interpretively, as well as Empson's delight in the "heresy of paraphrase." "Close reading," for Thaventhiran, is not a single practice leading inevitably to the New Critics. Her supposition that all her critics are empiricists implies, however, that they offer different ways of seeing the same thing, the point that De Man faulted in Richards.[17] Nonetheless, her work contributes to current discussions of literary history and reading practices in which this book also participates. By including Woolf as a critic along with Eliot and Empson, this book widens the gender parameters of such discussions, as does Thaventhiran's inclusion of Moore, rather than offering again an exclusively masculine history of literary production and criticism in which progressive moves must be separated from regressive ones. A recent example of such procedures would be *Literary Criticism: A Concise Political History*, in which Joseph North joins many who have come before him in his conviction that Eliot offers no progressive agenda in work whose truth was revealed in the calcified conservatism of his later writing (he consigns Eliot to an appendix).[18] North locates a usable past in F. R. Leavis and especially in I. A. Richards, acknowledging the work of Eve Kosofsky Sedgwick, Lauren Berlant, and D. A. Miller merely in passing,

Yet, as I noted earlier, Leavis, along with contributors to *Scrutiny*, continued to promote Eliot's radical revision to the canon, elevating Donne above Milton, Jacobean tragedy above Shakespeare. Cleanth Brooks might be the end of North's all but inevitable regressive story that Eliot initiated, followed by misguided practices, all tied, for North, in their failed political understanding. In his preface to *The Well Wrought Urn*, which features a reading of Donne's "The Canonization," the source of the book's title, Brooks invokes Eliot as well as Richards.[19] The possibility of the unexpected, the inadequacy of determinate labels, was recently demonstrated by Jem Bloomfield in an essay that seeks to answer the question of why Agatha Christie, Ngaio Marsh, and P. D.

James make *The Duchess of Malfi* key to mysteries they wrote in the mid-twentieth century. Eliot's promotion of Jacobean tragedy, ostensibly on the model of Shakespeare, but effectively working to displace the canonical author, is Bloomfield's answer. When the reign of Elizabeth II was hailed as a second Elizabethan Renaissance, Jacobean tragedy — Eliot's Jacobean tragedy — served a dissident voice of political protest, even in the otherwise conservative practices of these three genre fiction writers, not to mention criticism written by Eliot after he had declared his royalism, Anglicanism, and classicism.[20]

As a strong counterexample to North, I would mention recent work by Simon During. In an even-handed assessment of Leavis, for instance, he praises the rare coherence of Leavis's institutional academic program for the study of English; its advocacy of a closed canon of texts doomed it. "At the very least," During concludes, Leavis's program "reminds us that what the discipline needs are strong and generalizable social reasons and motives for its existence, which are inclined to critique of the present, and that, certainly, need to be bound to the universal forces and conditions (such as human *life*) even as those reasons and motives turn out to stand in the way of its own claims autonomously and authoritatively to carry the literary heritage forward."[21] During points here to central issues this book tackles about "being of two minds," the relationships between the "universal forces" of life and the literary life that During metaphorizes and humanizes as a matter of inheritance. I argue, rather, that "life" itself is in question; being is not identical to human existence. We will have ceased to exist before our world does; when that happens, existence will presumably go on without life as we think we know it. The universe is supposedly expanding; at the same time our solar system is bound to implode much as it exploded into being.

I place such cosmic questions in the philosophical tradition of Heidegger. During broaches them in "The Philosophical Origins of Modern Literary Criticism," an essay
that opens with G. E. Moore and Bertrand Russell and
focuses on both Eliot and Richards. (Lytton Strachey and
Roger Fry also figure for him, both important for Woolf).[22]
During's complex story leads from an idealist metaphysics at
its end in F. H. Bradley, the subject of Eliot's Harvard philosophy dissertation, to heady questions about the relation
of language and thinking, of what is and what is said to be;
literary texts (and, for Wittgenstein, language and language
games) serve as exemplary objects of thought to focus these
questions. These contemporary developments in philosophy
in England were no doubt important to the development of
the literary criticism that concerns me in this book, but, as
Eliot's Aristotle citation reminds us, the resources of classical philosophy extend into the present. The 1920s was not
only a time when Cambridge philosophy sought out new
ways through metaphysical questions; it also was the time of
Being and Time.[23]

I would note here that the literary critical agenda that I
trace in this book has not been the focus of studies of the role
of early modern literature in Eliot and Woolf. The most recent book on Eliot and early modern literature, while aware
of Eliot's criticism, focuses rather on allusions to and uses
of early modern texts in his poetry; likewise Alice Fox's *Virginia Woolf and the Literature of the English Renaissance* is
almost exclusively about echoes of Shakespeare in Woolf's
novels.[24] In his book on Empson, Michael Wood's examples
of his critical practice are almost all early modern; Wood
first explains this by describing Empson as "a good disciple
of Johns Donne as Eliot saw him ('thought to Donne was an
experience')" (17). Wood's observation is certainly demon-

strated in his first chapter on Empson's poetry but won't explain much about how he read Shakespeare or Milton.

Empson offers an exceptional turn around this way of
thinking of early modern literature only as influences of the
literary practices of Eliot, Woolf, and Empson, scanting their
writing as literary critics. Both come together in Empson's
1931 essay "Virginia Woolf." Its opening sentence, "Shakespeare was like Nature; we have been saying it for three centuries," prompts him to ask whether "the same claim can
be made for Mrs Woolf," since novelists "have seldom been
called Nature in this sense."[25] Empson finally answers his
question negatively; only Shakespeare can be "like Nature."
The "peculiar attitude to feminism" (447) that he finds in A
Room of One's Own prompts Empson's conclusion; Woolf's
advocacy of androgyny belies an achievement (and limits)
that belong to her sex; Shakespeare's masculinity does not.
Woolf finally stands accused of a lack of the objective corol-
lary attached to her gender.

Before he ends there, Empson vigorously explores the
possibility that Woolf might have been another Shakespeare
(the premise and hope embodied in Judith Shakespeare).
Difficult passages in To the Lighthouse engage his attention.
Why, after Mrs. Ramsay's death, when the house is animated
not by human inhabitants but by the forces of nature, does
the shawl she had thrown over the boar's head in the room
where the children slept unfold "with a roar, with a rup-
ture, as after centuries of quiescence, a rock rends itself from
the mountain and hurls crashing into the valley"? Empson
answers: the extravagance of this comparison follows from
Woolf's initial description of the shawl as looking like a
bird's nest or a mountain. Mrs. Ramsay's shawl, "her most
domesticated and personal piece of matter," has become
"monstrous and inhuman, like a mountain, like matter in

astronomy" (445). The comparison, drawn by Woolf's narrative voice that does not belong to anyone, refers to a nature
that also exists impersonally, a zone of existence that does
not correspond to mortal life or to the social limits of female
domesticity. Mrs. Ramsay, dead and alive, also is connected
to the inhuman life of mountains, stars, and birds. In this
passage, Woolf is Shakespeare, not simply an author who
makes use of him. In *Being of Two Minds*, I place Woolf beside Eliot and Empson convinced that her critical insights,
especially as they bear on "monstrous and inhuman" life,
on how we mortals live with and in it, are as powerful as the
insights about what writing achieves that Eliot and Empson
formulated.

As a coda to this introduction I would mention some current discussions of early modern literature that build their
arguments about the period on modernist engagements
with early modern texts. Like this book, they participate in
current discussions of the kinds of thinking and feeling that
literature makes possible, topics that I engage throughout
this book. David Marno, in *Death Be Not Proud: The Art
of Holy Attention*, focuses on the Donne sonnet that titles
his book to explore how thinking past prepositional thought
led to the realization of being expressed in the theological
negation of negation "Death, thou shalt die" that the sonneteer experiences as the end of his thought.[26] Donne's poems don't simply "invite the phenomenological approach,"
Marno writes, they "are *already* phenomenologies" (34).
Their attentiveness is, at once, a passive waiting for and
upon a power not one's own and an active striving to push
one's thoughts beyond its limits (readers strain to follow the
same trajectory). Just as the resurrection promises a mysterious reunification of scattered limbs, the end of attention is
the gathering of scattered thoughts — all driven by bodily life

and its concerns — into the other life we also live. We arrive at the end of these sonnets at a place already given in which we are; the "advantage" thinking has over resurrection is that "experiences of attentiveness . . . belong to this life" (12).

Marno formulates Donne's experience as not "primarily one of emotion but of cognition" (3); religious belief is not a feeling but a thought of thinking: "Donne's poems represent the process of seeking faith by making the reader experience what it feels like to think" (3). His phrasing of these cognitive relations seems a hair's breadth away from Eliot's claim in "The Metaphysical Poets" that "a thought to Donne was an experience; it modified his sensibility" (287), a phrase that appears in a footnote in Marno, largely where Eliot appears in his book, for example when he claims that "the story of modern professionalized literary criticism begins with the rediscovery of Donne" (28). As with North, Marno credits Richards, thanks to a discussion of one of Donne's holy sonnets in *Practical Criticism*, with the recognition of "the purpose of Donne's poems as spiritual exercises" (29).

Marno's arguments about Donne's procedures and ours, his positing of connections between early modern thinking (religious and philosophical, Descartes included) and modern practices of close reading and phenomenological explorations of existence, are comparable to Daniel Juan Gil's arguments in *Fate of the Flesh*.[27] Their archives of early modern and modern contexts differ (Gil's focus is sociological), but their literary interests correspond. Gil mentions Eliot several times as he explores early modern religious beliefs that ran counter to the usual supposition that, at death, body and soul separate; he excavates beliefs in which no body/soul split occurred; death took both soul and body and both regained life in the glorified body at the end of time. Some poets, Herbert and Vaughan especially, Donne less consistently so for Gil, testified to having that experience in this life, of being attached here and now to that other life to come (the experience Marno finds at the end of Donne's holy sonnets). Gil connects this scenario to zombie films as well as Eliot's night-of-the-living-dead scenario in "Tradition and the Individual Talent" when "the most individual parts" of a modern poet's "work may be those in which the dead poets, his ancestors, assert their immortality most vigorously" (14). Gil comments on how "the alien power of . . . bodily life" that Eliot imagines the object of thought in metaphysical poetry operates in the service of "using poetry as praxis, as equipment for living a new life . . . with one another and with the natural world in profound ways" (63, 190). It involves an existence that exceeds and yet also is ours. In *Feeling Faint*, Giulio Pertile considers a similar doubling of mind and life in early modernity. His main literary examples come from Montaigne, Spenser, and Shakespeare; in them, consciousness coincides with its loss, the realization that one's body, its feelings, its sensations, have a life of which one is otherwise oblivious. *De Anima*, which raises questions of life and mind for Eliot (for Agamben, too), is among the philosophical texts, early modern and modern, that Pertile explores in which the question of life (and death) is tied to the existence of the soul.[28] That other life is the one we find in literature.

1
Impersonal Eliot

"Tradition and the Individual Talent"

"Criticism is as inevitable as breathing"

In the opening paragraphs of "Tradition and the Individual Talent," T. S. Eliot urges his English readers to reconsider their attitudes toward tradition, questioning both the use of the term as a mode of "censure" and its weakly "approbative" archaeological deployment (13).[1] He contrasts these English predilections with contrary suppositions about French attitudes that he seems to support; while conceding to the English the possibility that French writing may be lacking in spontaneity, he does not endorse English dismissals of French critical intelligence. Making these comparisons, Eliot countenances differences in what he terms "race" and "nation," including himself in a "we" that seems to locate himself on the English side of these divisions even though he also seems not entirely to belong there. "We are such unconscious people," he notes parenthetically, consciously registering a division in the "we." Indeed, consciousness-raising seems to be his goal: "We might remind ourselves that criticism is as inevitable as breathing, and that we should be none the worse for articulating what passes in our minds when we read a book and feel an emotion about it, for criticizing our own minds in their work of criticism" (13–14).

These opening gestures of identification (and disidentification) rest on the asserted inevitable connection between criticism and breathing. Although it is true enough that as long as we are breathing we are likely capable of thinking, breathing is not inevitable; in fact, just the opposite. We all die. Perhaps it would be a mistake to recall that inevitability, just as it might be to think of thorns when a poet conjures up the rose as a symbol of love and beauty. Eliot's "reminder" seems literally aimed at re-minding. Somehow, a discussion about the subjects that title the essay, having been reframed as questions about criticism — about thinking and feeling — get reconsidered as a matter of life and breath. In this way Eliot counters both the refusal of "tradition" as a value and an archeological endorsement that consigns tradition to a past that is necessarily past. While we may think we value literature for the poet's individuality, Eliot concludes the second paragraph of his essay with an only slightly hedged counterclaim: "The most individual parts of his work may be those in which the dead poets, his ancestors, assert their immortality most vigorously" (14).

Some kind of life besides the one that requires us to be breathing seems involved in this claim about immortality, something perhaps akin to the reminder of consciousness in our unconsciousness that Eliot enjoins. This life, we are being asked to recognize, is not exactly ours. An essay that seemed to be addressing readers has become one about writers and the kinds of consciousness they have or about the kind of consciousness to which they have access in writing poems that draw our proper critical approbation, whether or not we realize how they do that. Poets seem to do it through their relation to dead ancestors who somehow are their life — or, rather, are the life of the poems they write. Eliot's initial notions of belonging couched in terms of race and nation in his English/French comparison seem also to be in question in the kind of ancestry that he proposes and the kind of life it entails — that is, if "immortality" is a kind of life, if poetic ancestry actually bears comparison with the ordinary temporal terms of human genealogy.

To accommodate questions like these, Eliot proceeds to describe the temporality of tradition, almost immediately rescinding what he seemed to be claiming about the way the dead do not remain dead. Tradition, Eliot now asserts, "cannot be inherited" (14); rather, labor is involved. The critical labor initially endorsed for the reader is now renamed as the poet's. To be a poet one must have — have developed — "the historical sense." That "sense" is not entirely sensible, if by that term we mean the kinds of sensations we have that tell us we are alive and breathing, perhaps alive and thinking too. Eliot's historical sense "involves a perception, not only of the pastness of the past, but of its presence." So, one must write "not merely with his own generation in his bones": here "his own" seems both to mean writing as someone living in the present and as someone self-generating in the present. The writer, Eliot continues, must also write "with a feeling that the whole of the literature of Europe from Homer and within it the whole of the literature of his own country has a simultaneous existence and composes a simultaneous order" (14). Eliot's "historical sense" challenges the ordinary temporal terms of history; so too his demarcations of race and nation seem to dissolve in this vision of the totality of literary history and of history tout court into a hegemony marked as European and presumed as male territory as well.[2] (These are among the parts of Eliot's consciousness-raising claims of which he remains unconscious.)

Thus far, the claims of the past on the present could seem like some night-of-the-living-dead scenario. To counter that, the simultaneity he posits opens the possibility of its reversal, for Eliot aims by resuscitating tradition to usher in the possibility of "the really new" (15) in the place of the old. This is the gist of what he labels his "preposterous" claim that the new work that fits into the tradition will be one that allows for the rewriting of tradition. The present makes the past as much as the past makes the present. Indeed, as Eliot moves to conclude the first section of his essay, he asserts that the advantage of the present over the past lies in knowing the past. We now have, it seems, more consciousness. So much so, Eliot ends, that it is not really necessary for the poet to be the kind of critical drudge he seemed to be prescribing as he laid out how much the poet needed to know to succeed. For there is the example of Shakespeare's remarkable ability to absorb so much from so little reading. And there is, perhaps even more to the point, what Eliot calls the poet's "necessary receptivity and necessary laziness" (17). The poets of the past may assert themselves, but somehow the supine receivers, through "continual surrender," are the winners in this historical exchange.

We have come, it seems, some distance from the inevitable connection between the exercise of critical intelligence and life as evidenced by breathing. We arrive at what Eliot claims as "a principle of aesthetic, not merely historical, criticism" (15). As this phrasing suggests, this "principle" claims absolute priority even as it remains in relation to what it is "not merely," what Eliot had called a "historical sense." More than one kind of life is involved. "The poet must be very conscious of the main current," Eliot avers (16). This does not mean what the rest of his essay seems to imply,

that the main current that begins with Homer only includes
writers like Aeschylus, Dante, Shakespeare, and Keats, the
only writers of the past explicitly named in the essay as exemplary. Eliot explains further that the "main current . . . does
not at all flow invariably through the most distinguished
reputations." How to achieve the "self-sacrifice, a continual
extinction of personality" necessary to join this current, is
the topic to which Eliot promises to turn in the next section
of the essay. In a piece of writing that looks like it is making
an argument, but at the same time continually rescinds it,
reframing its claims in just the way a poet needs — not in
arguments and terms "put into a useful shape for examina-
tions, drawing-rooms, or the still more pretentious modes
of publicity" (17) — it is perhaps no surprise that what Eliot promises to complete his task is "a suggestive analogy."[3]
Analogies are comparisons that entail at once likeness and
difference. The one Eliot proposes explores aesthetic life as
a science experiment.

"A bit of finely filiated platinum"

Eliot's analogy involves the catalysis that takes place when a
thread of platinum is inserted in a vessel of oxygen and sulfur dioxide: "They form sulphurous acid" (18). "The mind
of the poet is the shred of platinum," Eliot explains. In the
catalysis, while oxygen and sulfur dioxide are substantially
transformed, the platinum is not. It remains "unaffected . . .
inert, neutral and unchanged." So, too, does the mind of
the poet; yet, however "inert" it is, merely "present" at the
event, it nonetheless occasions it; its creative function stays
intact. The two chemical elements, in Eliot's analogy, represent emotions and feelings that may well affect the poet as a
man, but not the poet as a poet. The poet, the more perfect
he is, will "digest and transmute the passions which are its

material." Digesting and transmuting begin to describe the activity of this passive filament. Its materials are "particular words or phrases or images"; these are reshaped to provide the aesthetic experience delivered in the poem that provides the reader with "an experience different in kind from any experience not of art"; Eliot calls this, later in this section of the essay, a "new art emotion" (20). By the time the analogy is fully worked through, the mind "is in fact a receptacle for seizing and storing up numberless feelings, phrases, images, which remain there until all the particles can unite to form a new compound are present there" (19). Rather than simply being "present" in the chamber to enable the catalysis, the mind seems to be the chamber in which catalysis takes place; exceeding its earlier description as the one who digests, now it seizes its materials. It seems to be the place where the transformation occurs rather than being "present" in the chamber for it to happen. Where and how joining of the particles into something takes place remains elusive.

Eliot does not address such questions. Instead, he offers a series of literary examples in which feelings and emotions, or perhaps one or the other, or perhaps some word, or image, or phrase, result in pieces of writing that, despite their "great . . . variety," will all display "the intensity of the artistic process, the pressure, so to speak, under which the fusion takes place that counts" (19). Without naming the specific elements (emotions, words) in each of the examples he adduces, claiming for each of them proximity to or distance between the supposed emotion to be found in Dante's Ulysses or his Paolo and Francesca, Shakespeare's Othello or the Agamemnon of Aeschylus and the "artistic emotion" conveyed, Eliot concludes that "the difference between art and the event is always absolute" (19). It is marked by intensity, fusion, and transmutation. No passages are cited or specified to demonstrate the point. The emotions in Keats's "Nightingale Ode" "have nothing particular to do with the nightingale," his paragraph ends; the nightingale "because of its attractive name, and . . . its reputation" merely serves to bring them together. The poet doesn't have "a 'personality' to express, but a particular medium . . . in which impressions and experiences combine" (20). This conclusion pairs with Eliot's opening premise about an "Impersonal theory of poetry" (18) in which the poem is conceived within the "living whole" (17) of all poetry. To write such a poem, the poet's mind is "a more finely perfected medium." The poem in the poet's mind, it appears, lives an out-of-body experience reembodied in the "living whole" of tradition. The reader who receives the poem needs to realize that just as the nightingale is a poetic trope, the names of characters in Dante or Shakespeare likewise do not refer to real living beings but to poetic existences. The poet who created them lives a poetic life offered to his reader as the aesthetic experience of an art emotion.

F. W. Bateson stresses this point about aesthetic existence in an essay published some fifty years ago on the occasion of the fiftieth anniversary of the publication of "Tradition and the Individual Talent."[4] "The aesthetic state, because it is available to all of us, requires something like anonymity in the artist aiming to make it available," he writes (634); rather than speaking the idiolect of personal experience, the poet speaks within the medium of poetic language. Summoning up Saussure's distinction, Bateson makes the provocative suggestion that the language of the poem is not *parole* but *langue*, synchronic, not diachronic; it mobilizes the resources of language rather than ordinary usage.

Bateson offers some diachronic specifics about the original publication of Eliot's essay to explain why the passage on catalysis in "Tradition and the Individual Talent" casts a blot on its aesthetic goal. Noting that the essay originally appeared in two installments of *The Egoist* in the fall of 1919, Eliot's analogy functions as a "surprise ending" (631) to part one meant to guarantee the reader's return for the end.[5] Bateson deplores "the notorious episode of the 'finely filiated platinum'" (631), recommending that "the platinum episode is best skipped." Read without it, "the essay will be immediately recognized as probably the most original single critical essay that Eliot ever wrote" (632). Bateson's language gets heated: "notorious" is followed with "annoying and embarrassing" as he sniffs out what Eliot is up to in "blandly" summoning up "the stinks master's *catalysis*," rubbing our noses in it "with remorseless thoroughness" (632). Bateson holds his nose.

Michael Snediker has underscored the "sexual" implications in Bateson's response. Does the sulfuric smell of the chemistry class suggest some schoolboy fart joke? Snediker notices that the first literary example that Eliot offers to support his "stinks class" demonstration is a scene from *Inferno* xv; in it Dante discovers his old schoolmaster, the rhetorician and poet Brunetto Latini, in the circle of sodomites.[6] Snediker finds a linguistic key joining the poet's "preposterous" arsy versy place in literary history and Eliot's deployment of "filiated" to describe the filed-down platinum thread: "Sapient classicist that he was, Eliot might have known that 'filiated' derives from the Latin nouns 'filius' or 'filia,' and not the neuter 'filum'" (34). Eliot's "filiated" brings together poetic generation with biological reproduction; literal filiation becomes a metaphorical affiliation in which the difference between gender and the neuter is itself neutered into the possibility of both that also cancels the difference between them.[7] Rewriting filiation, Brunetto twice addresses Dante as his son, "figliuol" (xv.31, 37); Dante, in turn, acknowledges the teaching of his paternal master: "la

cara e buona imagine paterne/di voi quando nel mondo
ad ora ad ora/m'insegnavate come l'uom s'eterna" (83–85;
"the dear and kind paternal image of you when many a
time in the world you taught me how man makes himself
immortal").[8]

In his comment on this encounter, Eliot does not quote
these lines; he refers only to "a working up of the emotion
evident in the situation" (18). The feelings he has in mind
are perhaps encapsulated in the first words that Dante
speaks to his former teacher: "Siete voi qui, ser Brunetto"
(xv.30). Dante expresses surprise and regret at finding Brunetto among the sodomites. His reaction is not unwarranted;
no records exist that support that he was a sodomite, a claim
often made about schoolmasters, but not, so far as we know,
about this one.[9] Dante's surprise is not just his; it is ours,
too. Eliot may not have known that putting Brunetto Latini
in the circle of the sodomites was likely Dante's invention,
his rewriting of tradition, but his comment on the end of
the canto approaches it: "The last quatrain gives an image,
a feeling attached to an image, which 'came,' which did not
develop simply out of what precedes, but which was probably in suspension in the poet's mind until the proper combination arrived for it to add itself to" (18–19). Here are the
lines Eliot has in mind:

Poi si rivolse, e parve di coloro
       Che corrono a Verona il drappo verde
       Per la campagna; e parve di costoro
quelli che vince, non colui che perde.

                                                     (xv.121–24)

(Then he turned about and seemed like one of those
that run for the green cloth in the field at Verona,
and seemed not the loser among them, but the
winner.)

Eliot's praise of the final image performs a turn akin to
Dante's double take at finding his teacher among the sodomites. Brunetto's dangerous teaching, "how man makes
himself immortal," echoes Eliot's lesson about the "immortal" life of the poet. In his final words to Dante, Brunetto
hopes that Dante will commend "il mio Tesoro" (his *Treasure*, a poem of his that may have inspired Dante's *Comme-
dia*) "nel qual io vivo ancora" (119–20). This is the book in
which he still lives. He lives this life, too, in Dante's poem,
as Dante does as Brunetto's fine filiation. In Eliot's analogy,
the "finely filiated" platinum thread figures poetic life in
and as a "finely perfected medium." The reiteration of "fine"
in these phrases points, in fine, to the end that "comes" after.
Brunetto Latini, dead and yet alive, is not the loser, but the
winner of the race. Eliot inscribed himself in this genealogy
when he wrote the Italian words in which Dante's Brunetto
speaks to him of the *Tesoro*, the book in which he now lives,
in presentation copies of his own books.[10]

Dante recast the wished end of his *Inferno* encounter
with the sodomites in *Purgatorio* xxvi. There he meets his
poetic forebears Guido Guinizelli and Arnaut Daniel. He
hails Guinizelli as "il padre/mio e delli altri miei miglior"
(father of me and of others my betters; xxvi. 97–98), those
who have been inspired by his "sweet lines . . . which so
long as the modern use shall last will make their ink still
dear" (112–14).[11] Guinizelli turns temporal filiation into the
contemporaneity of Dante's desire, calling him a brother,
pointing to Arnaut Daniel as his forebear and the leader of
the confraternity. Answering Dante's desire, Arnaut Daniel
speaks to him. "Poi s'ascose nel foco che li affina," the canto
ends (xxvi.148); Daniel leaves; "He hides himself in the refining fire," another scene of poetic life as catalysis.

Eliot made that scene of poetic creation his own when he
borrowed from the Provencal Dante had Daniel speak to title

a version of his 1920 collection of poems *Ara Vos Prec*; the final line from *Purgatorio* xxvi appears toward the close of *The
Waste Land* (l.426). In *Little Gidding*, the "familiar compound ghost" (2.42) ends by prescribing "that refining fire"
(2.92). In its earliest draft, the speaker of these lines had been
greeted with these words: "Are you here, Ser Brunetto." Eliot revised the address; Dante's master became "*you*" (2.45),
a compound figure for the place of a contemporary poet in
dialogue with the living dead made to speak again.[12] Speaker
and spoken to are composite, compound figures who speak
"a double part" in a dialogue of you and I that takes place
in "the recurrent end of the unending" (2.27); this is a meeting of the familiar and the strange "in concord at this in-
tersection time/Of meeting nowhere, no before and after"
(2.53–54), a time that is no time taking place in no place.

Eliot recalled writing this passage in *Little Gidding* in
his 1961 essay "To Criticize the Critic," where he draws a
distinction between influence and imitation, enjoining only
the former: "influence can fecundate, whereas imitation —
especially conscious imitation — can only sterilize" (18).[13]
He immediately adds a parenthetical remark: "(But when I
came to attempt one brief imitation of Dante I was fifty-five
years old and knew exactly what I was doing)." In his 1950
talk "What Dante Means to Me," he explains how, in writing a passage meant "to be the nearest equivalent to a canto
of the Inferno and the Purgatorio," he solved the problem
of matching Dante's terza rima by "a simple alternation of
unrhymed masculine and feminine terminations as the
nearest way of giving the light effect of the rhyme in Italian" (128). What would threaten sterilization for the young
poet is answered in this cross-sexual coupling. Eliot's solution recalls what Guido Guinizelli says of himself and his
companions: "Our sin was hermaphrodite" ("nostro peccato
fu ermafroditi"; *Purgatorio* xxvi.82); threatened sterilization

becomes fecundity, a catalytic conversion. The fires that
burned in the hell of personality become the refining fires
of poetic existence.

"The poor benefit of a bewildering minute"

Eliot offers one more example to help his readers elucidate
the catalytic process of poetic creation. He introduces it this
way: "I will quote a passage which is unfamiliar enough to
be regarded with fresh attention in the light — or darkness —
of these observations" (20). In presenting this passage as
possibly illuminating or furthering the obscurity of his argument, Eliot's double gesture recalls how his essay moves,
rescinding itself to progress, erasing its terms of legibility to
advance the kind of new consciousness, new thinking, proposed. The example about to be offered is at once "unfamiliar" and at the same time capable of being regarded, looked
at again, as if familiar enough to provoke a second look. This
is the only passage of poetry quoted in Eliot's essay. Here are
the lines as Eliot quotes them:

> *And now methinks I could e'en chide myself*
> *For doating on her beauty, though her death*
> *Shall be revenged after no common action.*
> *Does the silkworm expend her yellow labours*
> *For thee? For thee does she undo herself?*
> *Are lordships sold to maintain ladyships*
> *For the poor benefit of a bewildering minute?*
> *Why does yon fellow falsify highways,*
> *And put his life between the judge's lips,*
> *To refine such a thing — keeps horse and men*
> *To beat their valours for her? . . .* (20)

Eliot presents a text without a title or author — in effect, an
anonymous piece of writing, as if it were at once new and yet

capable of being recognized as old, as if, perhaps, written by
Eliot. Certainly, as Eliot goes on to describe it as "a combination of positive and negative emotions," it answers to the
back-and-forth preposterous writing we have been reading.
Telling us that its "combination" of positive and negative
would be "evident" if the passage were "taken in its context," Eliot gives no context for the passage — unless "Tradition and the Individual Talent" is that. He alludes to "the
dramatic situation to which the speech is pertinent," which
hints at the genre of the citation, but also says that, were we
to know what that situation was, it would be "inadequate" to
an understanding of the "balance" that the passage achieves.
Blanking the context and situation in the drama quoted, Eliot leaves us with the "art emotion" of the passage; to read it,
the passage must stand alone, decontextualized. Yet within
"Tradition and the Individual Talent" it exemplifies the "art
emotion" the essay theorizes.

The text Eliot cites belongs to the "main current . . .
which does not at all flow invariably through the most distinguished reputations" (16). It is not by Dante or Shakespeare,
its author as obscure as Eliot was as a poet in 1919. Some
readers then might have recognized the lines; they come
from a Jacobean play, *The Revenger's Tragedy* (1607); Eliot
cites it from the Mermaid edition edited by John Addington
Symonds, in print from 1888 on: the phrase, "a bewildering
minute," is unique to that edition of the play.

Eliot's citation would become less obscure to readers after
his interventions into literary history, among them a number
of essays on early modern English drama published over the
next fifteen years, eventually gathered into the volume of
Eliot's selected essays. Eliot's short-lived advocacy of these
texts was furthered by F. R. Leavis and his followers with
long-lasting effect; editions of *The Revenger's Tragedy* up to
the present almost invariably gloss the lines of the play Eliot

quotes with his remarks about them.[14] The lines also served Eliot as touchstones in a number of his essays. In "Philip Massinger" (1920), Eliot faults that playwright's empty linguistic facility against the passage cited from *The Revenger's Tragedy* as well as a couple of lines from *The Changeling*: "These lines of Tourneur and Middleton exhibit that perpetual slight alteration of language, words perpetually juxtaposed in new and sudden combinations, meanings perpetually *eingeschachelt* into meanings, which evidences a very high development of the senses, a development of the English language which we have perhaps never equalled."[15] The lines about the silkworms and the highwayman exhibit "a gift for combining, for fusing into a single phrase, two or more diverse impressions," Eliot writes (209), using key terms in "Tradition and the Individual Talent" to describe the lines. The characteristic back and forth that can make Eliot's own writing seem to be acts of evasion and mystification might well be located in the linguistic achievement he finds in these Jacobean texts. In them fleeting and disparate sense impressions acquire or reveal some otherwise unperceived relationship that attaches them to each other.

In his 1932 essay on John Ford, Eliot praises *The Revenger's Tragedy* as "all that can be accomplished within the limits of a single play" (203), an achievement limited only when compared to the entirety of Shakespeare's ouevre. Such transmutations of life into art serve a different sense of what "life" might mean. "A 'living' character is not necessarily 'true to life,'" Eliot writes (212), performing a seachange from "living" to "life." In that respect Marston is said to exceed the accomplishment of "the author of *The Revenger's Tragedy*" (230). Despite the unintelligibility of his language (or perhaps because of it), Marston breaks through to "some other plane of reality" (229), a "double reality . . . the sense of something behind, more real than any of his personages and their action" (230). This "something" Eliot finds too in Ben Jonson — "the creation of a world" (156). "It is not human life that informs Envy and Sylla's ghost," he remarks about characters in *Cataline*, "but it is energy of which human life is only another variety" (151). That other world — aesthetic totality — gives access to an unperceived aspect in the reality we ordinarily take to be real. To express the relationship of the two requires language that works at the level of its potentiality (*langue*, as Bateson suggested) from which more ordinary communication (*parole*) arises; this is language whose unintelligibility opens the possibility of a new understanding. (It is not the "drama of common life" [181], of "ordinary people in ordinary life" [175] that Eliot deplored in Thomas Heywood's plays.) In his 1930 essay on Tourneur, Eliot credits "the death motive . . . the loathing and horror of life itself" for the accomplishment of *The Revenger's Tragedy*: "To have realized this motive so well is a triumph; for the hatred of life is an important phase — even, if you like, a mystical experience — in life itself" (190). The "bewildering moment" might well be one in which one tries to grasp the doubleness of a moment inevitably evanescent and at the same time part of a life that exceeds it. We all die, yet life continues. Negation and affirmation meet in the energy of a "double reality" of "living" and "life."

Frank Kermode has fastened on the phrase "a bewildering moment" as key for Eliot, noting its echo in several of his poems, exploring how Eliot draws on it in a 1935 letter to Stephen Spender to summarize poetic experience.[16] There Eliot details three stages in a poet's reading experience: it begins in "surrender" to an author: "You have to give yourself up, and then recover yourself, and the third moment is having something to say." As Kermode suggests, this process parallels the potential author's relation to tradition in "Tradition and the Individual Talent," the extinction of per-

sonality that is followed by the creation of the artwork. For
Eliot's third stage, Kermode recalls not the "art emotion"
but the "objective correlative" Eliot found lacking in *Hamlet* and requisite for the text to do more than arise from the
confounded emotion of an initial overwhelming attraction.
Kermode summarizes its nature in the cited lines from *The
Revenger's Tragedy*: "a mortuary eroticism balancing on the
moment of simultaneous enchantment and loss, the sexual
surrender" (13). His discussion seems only to be about the
emotional experience of an author, his emotional surrender followed by "intellectual engagement" (15) that delivers
the "single thought of the permanence that underlies all
change" (16).

Kermode's dualistic readings of Eliot turn "correlation"
into replacement of one reality for another; when emotion becomes thought it ceases to be emotion. His "single
thought" equates Eliot's early critical position with his later
declarations of political, religious, and artistic conformity,
binding him to "external authority" (18). In the "preposterous" temporality of "Tradition and the Individual Talent,"
however, before and after are reversed into a new simultaneity, a nondualistic two-in-oneness in which original attachments are sustained, transmuted, correlated. At the end of
his essay on Tourneur, Eliot noted that "*Bewildering* is the
reading of the 'Mermaid' text," uniquely there, not to be
found in other editions better founded on textual evidence:
"It is a pity if they be right, for *bewildering* is much the richer
word here" (192).[17] The richness of "bewilderment" lies in
the combination it achieves, erecting a law on one's impressions and effacing that origin at the same time. I would
note the proper name "Wilde" at the core of this bewitching word.

Eliot preferred Symonds's emendation of bewitching into
bewildering, perhaps because it lacks the gendered impli-

cation of female agency or feminization of male agency. In explaining the positive/negative force of the lines, he describes it as "an intensely strong attraction toward beauty and an equally intense fascination by the ugliness which is contrasted with it and which destroys it" (20). "Beauty" here effaces "her beauty," making the erotic encounter more like the aesthetic experience Kermode describes. The ugliness that opposes beauty seems to be "her death," but perhaps also the death of the speaker of these lines, who would "chide" himself "for doating on her beauty." Perhaps her death and his are involved as is indicated by the use of "for" in this passage.[18] As in Eliot poems where "you" and "I" are as often as not an internal couple, here too the "I" that opens these lines — "And now methinks I could e'en chide myself" — is doubled in self-reflexive castigation, as if some force not himself was impersonally chiding himself. Death might well do that.

To illustrate the process, the speaker, much like Eliot as he moved from the first to the second part of his essay, provides us with analogies; all of them, however dissimilar, suggest transformation, this for that. Silkworms kill themselves to make silk. The ones in these lines are gendered female: "For thee does she undo herself?" Who is the "thee" here? The "I" self-addressed or the one who survives in the lines? Crossings continue in the exchange of "lordships" and "ladyships," two words that look like they might be equivalents; in them male property also is lost, "sold" to pay for "ladyships," money for a whore perhaps paid for with male potency. It's as if male arousal was his female undoing (the speaker might have learned this from Hamlet). Perhaps something like this is involved in the obscure analogy about the "fellow" who falsifies highways and puts "his life between the judge's lips," as if the highway were a public road made dangerous by illegitimate reproduction; the judge's lips might be where the ill-considered business transacted "for the poor benefit of a bewildering minute" occurs. (Perhaps the fellow has put into the judge's lips the same bodily part he had forced into the woman's body.) The end of this activity — of this life, of this poem — aims "to refine such a thing," to accomplish the transmutive activity of the refining fire. Eliot concludes that the "whole effect" of the lines (the effects that make a new whole) "is due to the fact that a number of floating feelings, having an affinity to this emotion by no means superficially evident, have combined with it to give us a new art emotion." "Affinity" itself seems affiliated with the "finely filiated" poetic mind at work in the poem. The lines enact analogies for the process through which poems are made. "Affinity" suggests a connection that continues even as it is worn down to a thread, delivering something not evident except as it offers itself to "us." In the receipt of these lines we have a poetic experience. Because the speaker has doubled himself (undoing himself and reconstituting himself in his words), we are capable of being included in the "you" to whom this I speaks.

Eliot had offered conflicting advice about contextualizing these lines: although their emotions are said to be "evident" in context, its "art emotion" has an "affinity . . .by no means superficially evident" in the drama at hand. It seems useful at least to recall that Vindice, the speaker of these lines in *The Revenger's Tragedy*, carries with him, as he has from the opening of the play, the skull of his dead beloved Gloriana; he addresses it in his self-address to us. Dressed up for the occasion, the skull is meant to attract the Duke (he was responsible for her death). When the Duke kisses the skull he will suck poison from it. His death will reenact hers, her seduction reverse his. Death and life cross as the skull comes alive to kill; sexual attraction, rather than life-giving, gives death. In an essay on *The Revenger's Tragedy* and Walter Benjamin's account of the *Trauerspiel*, Martin Moraw underlines Benjamin's claim about the skull, that genre's most significant prop: "This is the form in which man's subjection to nature is most obvious and it significantly gives rise not only to the enigmatic question of the nature of human existence as such, but also of the biographical historicity of the individual."[19]

Benjamin links these questions of life and its meaning to the characters whose allegorical names in *Trauerspiel* are signifiers emptied of transcendental meaning. Vindice speaks to a skull in which beauty and ugliness come together, a you who is also the inevitable end of the I, an idealized and debased beloved that reflects the acts of a lover-revenger, whose name names a part that is not his alone. Many of the characters in *The Revenger's Tragedy* have such allegorical, generic names; most lack proper names, named instead by their family or social positions — Duke, Younger Brother. As Jeremy Lopez points out, such nominations render characters anonymous, interchangeable; all are caught in the trammels of self/other destruction — the plot line of revenge.[20] "Brother," the most frequent of these, points this affinity and affiliation. When we read the text, we find the names Supervacuo or Spurio, but in performance, all we hear is "brother" repeated. All of them have in common the death that ensues.

Through such erasures of the proper name, Lopez's essay aims to restore *The Revenger's Tragedy* to the anonymous status it had in its first printing; he argues against its recent reassignment to Thomas Middleton, a question of the authorship of the play of which Eliot was aware; in "Cyril Tourneur" (1930), written as a review of a new edition of Tourneur, Eliot applauded Allardyce Nicoll's rejection of "E. H. C. Oliphant's theory that Middleton authored *The Revenger's Tragedy*" (184), an ascription that he also proclaims "brilliant" (186). In "Thomas Heywood" (1931), a reference to some lines by Middleton leads Eliot to offer them "as proof that Middleton wrote *The Revenger's Tragedy*" (178), while in his essay on Ford (1932), he refers to "the author of *The Revenger's Tragedy*, whether we call him Tourneur or Middleton" (203). Finally, in "John Marston" (1934), Eliot's indifference leaves us simply with the unnamed "author of *The Revenger's Tragedy*" (230).

It is with that undoing that Eliot concludes the second section of "Tradition and the Individual Talent," attempting again, finally, to put to rest any notion that personal emotion motivates the poem whose aim is "to express feelings which are not in actual emotions at all" (21). There is, it seems, not a trace of the subjective in the "objective correlative" to be delivered. Yet, if we were to imagine that the difference between art feelings and ordinary emotions lies in the conscious articulation that Eliot promoted at the opening of his essay, that does not appear to be the case detailed here. Arguing against the formulation for poetic creation in the Preface to the *Lyrical Ballads*, "emotion recollected in tranquility," Eliot's poetic "concentration" "does not happen consciously or of deliberation." Yet, there is verbally an unacknowledged affinity between "concentration" and "recollection," as there is in what emerges, "a new thing," for, of course, the poem is not the experience it turns into words. "These experiences are not 'recollected,'" Eliot insists, "they finally unite." Again, one wonders how different unity is from re-collecting. It is "not without distortion" that the final moment is one of tranquility, Eliot insists; it is "'tranquil' only in that it is a passive attending upon the event." We recognize this as the claim that ended the first part of the essay, on the poet's "necessary receptivity and necessary laziness" (17), or the characterization of the poet's mind in a bath of seething emotions remaining "inert, neutral, and unchanged" (18).

Eliot reformulated this scene of creation in later critical writing. In "The Three Voices of Poetry" (1953), the origin of the poem is not in "an emotion, in any ordinary sense," not in an idea, either, but rather an "obscure impulse" to give birth in response to an oppression demanding relief, the haunting of a "demon . . . against which he feels powerless." The poem is an exorcism, not a human communication, and its delivery is "something very near annihilation." When it's over the poet may "rest in peace." Something utterly new enters the world in this demon spawn. It does not belong to the poet. "What happens," Eliot said in his Charles Eliot Norton lecture on March 31, 1933, "is something *negative* . . . the breaking down of strong habitual barriers, an outburst of words which we hardly recognize as ours."[21]

Out of negation creation arises, *ex nihilo*, as it were; the project of effacement nonetheless depends upon the one who will be effaced in the process. Eliot gestures toward him (toward himself) as he ends this section of the essay, inviting our sympathetic identification with this figure, the necessary loser in the race he wins: "Poetry is not a turning loose of emotion, but an escape from emotion; it is not the expression of personality, but an escape from personality. But, of course, only those who have personality and emotions know what it means to want to escape from these things" (21).

ὁ δὲ νοῦς ἴσως θειότερόν τι καὶ ἀπαθές ἐστιν

The final paragraph-long section of "Tradition and the Individual Talent" opens with these Greek words. Eliot treats them even more radically than he does the citation from *The Revenger's Tragedy*; not only are they untranslated with no source indicated, not a word is said about them unless Eliot's opening remark is meant to do that: "This essay proposes to halt at the frontier of metaphysics or mysticism" (21). "A

reader untrained in Greek scansion might assume this to be
a line from Homer or that *Agamemnon* discussed earlier,"
Stan Smith notes, in an essay that explores the frontiers that
this Greek citation straddles.[22] Eliot is not alluding to such a
text, as Smith notes, but picking up on a metaphysical question raised just when he appeared to have finished with his
catalytic analogy: "The point of view which I am struggling
to attack is perhaps related to the metaphysical theory of
the substantial unity of the soul" (19). Eliot's citation comes
from Aristotle's *De Anima*; the substantial unity of the soul
is certainly a concern in it. *Nous*, mind, is the subject of
the sentence quoted (408b). Smith quotes it in the translation of J. A. Smith, an Oxford philosopher with whom Eliot
studied: "Mind is, no doubt, something more divine and
impassible." Aristotle's description of mind matches Eliot's
view of the poet's mind, "unaffected . . . inert, neutral, and
unchanged" (18) by its experience in the sulfuric vat of emotion (18). Aristotle's sentence compares mind to body. Eliot
associates the poet's mind with Mind, per se.

Eliot admits to a struggle over a theory of the soul, the
possibility that his impersonal poetic theory is "perhaps" related to the quandary Aristotle ponders: why does mental
facility seem to fade as the body ages? Are body and soul
a substantial unity? Smith's translation of the passage answers the question decisively: mind and body do not represent a "substantial unity" if mind is divine and impassible,
unaffected. Other translators of the passage are not so sure
that there is "no doubt" about this. In doubt, precisely, is
the meaning of ἴσως, the word that qualifies the assertion.[23]
H. Lawson-Tancred's translation allows "the possibility that
the mind is something more divine and unaffected," not
certainty; so does Mark Shiffman's: "But perhaps intellect
is something more divine and imperturbable." Joe Sachs

edges the sentence in Smith's direction: "The intellect is probably more divine and is unaffected." W. S. Hett more or less concurs: "Possibly the mind is too divine, and is therefore unaffected," while Fred D. Miller, Jr. similarly offers, "But thought is perhaps something more divine and unaffected."[24] Eliot's association of the poet's mind with "mind" in this citation does not resolve the question of the substantial unity of the soul.

Eliot pondered the question of Aristotelian substance in an essay that appeared in *The Monist* in October 1916, "The Development of Leibniz' Monadism." "Wherever Aristotle pursues the concept of substance, it eludes him," Eliot writes. "In one sense, the composite of form and matter . . . is substance; in another sense substance is 'the form by which the matter is some definite thing.'. . . Matter certainly is not substance, because matter has neither limit nor the potency of limit by separation." Moreover, he continues, "the same incoherence appears in his account of the soul. Is the substance the compound of matter and form, or the form alone?" Aristotle seems unable to solve the relationship of beings to Being.[25] As Eliot realizes, "For Aristotle reality is here and now; and the true nature of mind is found in the activity which it exercises. Attempt to analyze the mind, as a thing, and it is nothing. It is an operation" (195). Eliot's formulation of this Aristotelian aporia about the animating principle of soul by which the body lives and the mind thinks is strikingly close to his account of the poet's mind, whose receptive passivity becomes an activity. The passage from a state of attending, being present, to the writing of the poem looks mystical or metaphysical: nothing becomes something; something unmoved produces something new, a thought, a poem, an art emotion that remains present.

Eliot's formulations are strikingly in line with Giorgio

Agamben's explorations of the concept of potentiality in Aristotle and its relevance to human creativity. Agamben's essay "On Potentiality" takes off from a passage in *De Anima* in which Aristotle ponders the question of why the senses only seem operative — only seem to exist — when there is something to sense. There is no sensation of the senses themselves; sensation seems insensate when it is inactive (417a).[26] The answer is that sense must be potential, inoperative, for it to have the potential to act. Agamben radicalizes the point: it is *"the existence of non-Being"* that conditions the being of life" (179). In his essay on Heidegger's term "facticity," Agamben traces a route to Dasein that begins with Aristotle in order to arrive at the human condition of thrownness — powerlessness — rooted in our "constitutive non-originarity" (189). "All potentiality (*dynamis*)," Heidegger writes in his interpretation of Aristotle, "is impotentiality (*adyanamia*), and all capacity . . . is essentially passivity" (201). Human possibility, Agamben suggests in an essay on Derrida entitled *"Pardes,"* is "the potentiality that no one writes" (216). His authorization for this claim about the impersonality of the trace comes from *De Anima* 430a: "'The mind is like a writing tablet on which nothing is actually written'" (215).

In writing, nothing becomes something. Eliot's "Tradition and the Individual Talent," we have observed, proceeds by withdrawing, destabilizing whatever terms it offers; it continually remarks and demarks the boundaries of its "preposterous" territory. When it halts at the frontier of metaphysics and mysticism, it occupies a nowhere strongly resonant with the location of the ghost of Brunetto Latini in *Little Gidding*. This terrain Eliot nominates at the end of his essay as the "life of the poem"; its life is not the poet's but the life in which he must live "in what is not merely the present, but the present moment of the past," to be "conscious not of what is dead, but of what is already living" (22). These concluding words intimate the poet living consciously in what he cannot be conscious of, since it is what lives in the poem in which he is not; it lives before and after him but is not him. These mind-boggling propositions about the life of the mind — the *nous* in question in the sentence from *De Anima* that Eliot cites — are not just modern or postmodern aporias. In the glossary that he provided for his translation of *De Anima*, Mark Shiffman notes that Aristotle's coinage *entelecheia* (being-fully-itself) is fundamentally a definition of what the soul is: "Beings are alive . . . by actively maintaining those potencies in their potential for operating."[27]

In "What Is the Act of Creation?," Agamben writes about the joy he experiences when the work he contemplates leaves unsaid something that can be thought further.[28] It reveals at that moment the coincidence of the delivery of thought and the potential for further thought that remains a potential unexpressed, an "impersonal zone of indifference in which every proper name, every copyright, and every claim to originality fades away" (34). It opens that zone in which "every human potentiality is co-originally impotentiality," one in which the author shows "a relation with his own not-being and not-doing" (39). In "Dante" (1929), Eliot quotes passages from *Purgatorio* xvi and xvii about free will and the soul and the impetus of love. "It is not necessary to have traced the descent of the theory of the soul from Aristotle's *De Anima*," he writes, to appreciate the lines as poetry (261). In the first of his Clark lectures, Eliot defines metaphysical poetry as "work in which the thought is so to speak *fused* into poetry at a very high temperature."[29] Ronald Schuchard notes Eliot's figure for catalytic conversion in "*fused*"; he points a few pages later to Eliot's allusion to "the Thomist-Aristotelian theory of the origin and devel-

opment of the soul" (53) in Dante. These include lines in
Purgatorio xviii where Dante's Virgil discusses substantial
form (xviii.49) as distinct from matter and yet only operative there, and *Purgatorio* xxv, which introduces the concept
of "possible intellect" (xxv.65). Imagination, whose signifi-
cance was first articulated in *De Anima* III.3, had become,
by Dante's time, Agamben argues in *Stanzas*, the crucial
concept for exploring the relationship of the human mind
to "possible intellect," the capacity to imagine more than is
readily apparent. The image, "situated at the vertex of the individual soul, at the limit between individual and universal,
corporeal and incorporeal, . . . appears as the sole exhausted
spot of ash that the combustion of individual existence leaves
on the impassable and invulnerable threshold of the Separate and Eternal."[30] Agamben's language here catches up
Dante's meeting with Brunetto Latini and its poetic course
in the *Divine Comedy* and beyond as the life of Eliot's tradition. The fantasy-image moves on a "breath that animates
the universe" (94), a life that makes for connections beyond
individual life. The animating force of Dante's "dolce stil
novo" (*Purgatorio* xxiv.57), it requires the inspiration of love.
"Amor mi spira" (53); "spiro," Agamben notes, points to "the
pneumo-phantasmatic character of the process of love, . . .
the foundation of a theory of poetic language" (125). If we
were to return to Eliot's initial figuration of critical thinking
as breathing, it would be to this breath of life in thinking
itself. The foundation in the phantasmatic life of the poetic image rests on what Saussure articulated in declaring
that "in language there are only differences without positive
terms."[31] Poetic language seeks to inhabit "the original frac-
ture of presence that is inseparable from the Western experience of being" (136), the bar between signified and signifier
in Saussure's schema that divides and connects Being and
Nonbeing.

The Metaphysical Poets

Eliot's most decisive contribution to the project for "a really new" form of poetry that would answer to, yet also reshape, tradition lies in three essays on seventeenth-century poetry published in *TLS* in 1921. In the last of these to appear, "The Metaphysical Poets" (a review of H. J. C. Grierson's anthology, *Metaphysical Lyrics and Poems of the Seventeenth Century*), metaphysical poetry is declared to be in "the main current" (281), not, as more usually supposed, a digression from it. Eliot's revisitation of seventeenth-century poetry is couched in much the same terms as he offered in revaluing tradition in "Tradition and the Individual Talent." "Metaphysical poetry must no longer be heard as a term of abuse," he writes in the opening paragraph of "The Metaphysical Poets," nor should it be praised simply for its archaeological quaintness (281). Similarly, opening his essay on Andrew Marvell, written to celebrate the three-hundredth anniversary of his birth on March 31, 1621, Eliot sees the task of the critic "to bring the poet back to life" (292). The way to do that is to resuscitate what has never died, "to squeeze the drops of the essence" of the poems that convey a quality unknown to most now. These texts house "something permanently valuable, which subsequently disappeared, but ought not to have disappeared," he claims in "The Metaphysical Poets" (285). They represent "the direct and normal development of the precedent age," specifically its drama. Hence the citation from *The Revenger's Tragedy* in "Tradition and the Individual Talent"; at the end of "The Metaphysical Poets," lines from *The Revenge of Bussy d'Ambois* serve a similar purpose. Eliot links seventeenth-century poetry to the late nineteenth-century French poets Jules Laforgue and Tristan Corbière, his more immediate poetic inspirations. What was "direct and normal" will serve as a model for the

new. But to do so "the poet must become more and more
comprehensive, more allusive, more indirect, in order to
force, to dislocate if necessary, language into his meaning"
(289). The result of this violent dislocation of language — its
wrenching away from ordinary usage — resembles a metaphysical conceit. Recovery is not simply a return, but a rewriting in which what was "direct and normal" will look —
will be — "indirect," dislocated and relocated at once.

The most memorable central contention of "The Metaphysical Poets" was Eliot's claim that a "dissociation of sensibility" "set in" in the seventeenth century "from which we
have never recovered" (288, a thesis broached in his 1920
essay on Philip Massinger, whom he faulted as an initiator
of dissociation).[32] In dramatists — Eliot names Chapman,
Middleton, Webster, and Tourneur — and in Donne "intellect was immediately at the tip of the senses. Sensation became word and word was sensation" (210). Then came "the
period of Milton" and the fall from unified sensibility. (Eliot's historical myth is the subject of *Paradise Lost*.) In "The
Metaphysical Poets," Eliot couples Milton with Dryden as
"the two most powerful poets" who "aggravated" the dissociation (288).

Eliot concludes "The Metaphysical Poets" by again plac-
ing Donne and his ilk in "the direct current" (290) that requires, by indirect means, to be repaired. It requires a refusal
of the direct current that might lead modern poets to follow
Browning and Tennyson. "Something . . . happened to the
mind of England between the time of Donne or Lord Herbert of Cherbury and the time of Tennyson and Browning"
(287). Eliot terms it "the difference between the intellectual
poet and the reflective poet." What he seems to mean is the
difference between a poem that offers the immediacy of the
process of thinking and one in whose retrospective recollection thought is calcified and stopped. The poem that results

is lifeless; "poetic" becomes a synonym for anodyne and ho-
mogenized feelings whose main characteristic, as a citation
from William Morris in "Andrew Marvell" underscores, is
its vagueness when compared to "the more explicit reference of emotion to object" in Marvell (299). That conjunction produces true suggestiveness, poems that make possible
ongoing thought and the ongoing critical activity that keeps
them alive.

Such a conjunction of word and sensation is memorably captured in Eliot's pronouncement about Donne in
"The Metaphysical Poets": "A thought to Donne was an
experience; it modified his sensibility" (287). This sentence
suggests that ordinarily thinking and experiencing remain
separate. Much as in the opening of "Tradition and the Individual Talent," Eliot enjoins the making conscious of the
activity of mind that usually goes on unawares. How that
happens is, however, a bit difficult to parse, thanks to the
multiple possible meanings of sensibility, which range from
mere sensation to an intuitive understanding that can be
distinguished from ratiocination. Modification of sensibility,
moreover, suggests a lessening, rather than a heightening
of those powers, which also seem to preexist both thought
and experience. The sentence about Donne not only puts in
play the processes that unify sensibility; where that happens
is also in question. Does "Donne" here refer to the man or
to the part of him that writes poems? Even in the sentence
about his unified sensibility, it seems possible that Donne's
personality was not entirely effaced.

Eliot says as much in "Andrew Marvell" when he notes
that "Donne is difficult to analyse" (292); something that
appears "at one time a curious personal point of view" can
"at another time appear rather the precise concentration of
a kind of feeling diffused in the air about him. Donne and
his shroud and his motive for wearing it, are inseparable,

but they are not the same thing" (293). What drives Eliot back and forth, the seventeenth century "for more than a moment" brought together, gathering and digesting "into its art all the experience of the human mind which . . . the later centuries seem to have been partly engaged in repudiating" (293). Eliot softens the distinctions that he seemed to insist on in "The Metaphysical Poets" and ends by allowing that "Donne would have been individual at any time and place," contrasting him with Marvell, whose best poems are "the product of European, that is to say Latin, culture." When he comes to discuss "To His Coy Mistress," the poem to which he devotes most of his attention, it is to focus on it as a compendium "of the great traditional commonplaces of European literature" (295).

Donne and Marvell are both metaphysical poets, yet in "The Metaphysical Poets," Marvell is only mentioned as a name in a list — no poems of his are cited alongside the three examples from Donne presented in that essay (as well as citations from Henry King, Lord Herbert of Cherbury, and George Chapman); conversely, Donne is mentioned in "Andrew Marvell" only to distinguish his straddling the personal/impersonal divide in contradistinction to Marvell, who distills an "unknown quantity" (292); "whether we call it wit or reason, or even urbanity," it constitutes Marvell's "modest and certainly impersonal virtue" (304). These multiples — the string of possible names joined by "or" — the positing of Donne and Marvell in different degrees of relationship to tradition and the individual talent, characterize Eliot's thinking in these essays. In his pithiest and most memorable pronouncements, he can appear to be making strong, exclusionary statements, but everywhere absolute distinctions are looked at from multiple perspectives.

The first gesture in "The Metaphysical Poets," to define what that rubric means, Eliot declares "difficult" (282). Instead of a definition, he posits several kinds of metaphysical verse, explaining each by its origin: Donne's poems are said to be "late Elizabethan," most akin to Chapman; another branch of metaphysical poetry is "courtly" and stems from Jonson; a third is devotional, but also Elizabethan insofar as it too depends upon Italian, rather than Jonson's Latin models. Putting Chapman close to Donne a few pages later in the essay, Eliot writes, "In Chapman especially there is a direct sensuous apprehension of thought, or a recreation of thought into feeling, which is exactly what we find in Donne" (286). The "or" in this sentence is telling, since it equates, or substitutes, one process for another. In the first, which seems to describe the immediacy of seventeenth-century verse in contradistinction to what followed its dissociation, it is impossible to distinguish thought from its sensuous apprehension. In the second, thought becomes feeling and is recreated as it. Perhaps the latter only is what Eliot claims for Donne's "modified sensibility," or perhaps that description is yet another alternative way of apprehending the unification of consciousness. Keeping "or" in play allows for the crossing of categories.

By the end of "The Metaphysical Poets," all the poems that fall under that rubric are not merely in the "direct current" (290); they are no different from any serious poem at any time. That time-transcending sameness in no way contradicts all the ways in which Donne and Marvell are unmistakably themselves. Indeed, not just them: in "Andrew Marvell," at least, Eliot can enunciate a common property that joins Marvell's "Horation Ode" to Milton's *Comus* and some poems of Cowley; he calls it "wit" and defines it as "a tough reasonableness beneath the slight lyric grace" (293). That conjunction is rephrased later as "the aura around a bright clear centre" (300). The figures in each of these formulations exchange inside and outside; one kind of form replaces the other as a way to describe the animating force of poetic utterance. "It involves, probably, a recognition, implicit in the expression of every experience, of other kinds of experience which are possible" (303). Keeping in play the probable and the possible, Eliot's discussions remain within the orbit of *De Anima* in which the creative force in the created object exceeds any particular object in which it is manifest.

"Forming new wholes"

The paragraph in "The Metaphysical Poets" that sums up Donne's unified sensibility concludes by generalizing it as the quality of any genuine poet:

> When a poet's mind is perfectly equipped for its work, it is constantly amalgamating disparate experiences; the ordinary man's experience is chaotic, fragmentary. The latter falls in love, or reads Spinoza, and these two experiences have nothing to do with each other, or with the noise of the typewriter or the smell of cooking; in the mind of the poet these experiences are always forming new wholes. (287)

In these sentences Donne the man disappears into the mind of the poet; ordinary life is chaotic, fragmentary; the mind makes it into something coherent and unified. Poems come out of the poetic mind when it is in a state in which disparate experiences lose their specificity to find what relation they may have with each other. As in "Tradition and the Individual Talent," the image concretizes and amalgamates disparate experiences. Its singularity always is in relation to something with which it has an affinity — an affiliation — not an identity. "New wholes" emerge from the poetic process of image-making: continuous amalgamations, momentary for-

mulations, lyric utterances, pithy claims like the sentences
Eliot forges about Donne's thought as an experience, and
then rephrases as modified sensibility; two potentially different processes become one. To read Eliot's essays one must
stay alert to the mobility of thought as it exceeds one's grasp.
The making of "new wholes" is not the making of a whole;
thought remains in motion, thought as emotion. Definition is always indefinition. Citations are decontextualized
to make new configurations; amalgams stay still for only as
long as they are made. To stay with these acts of thinking
means to be kept thinking, to be mobilizing the creative
energy of one's mind, its capacity to be attuned to another
mind. For Eliot, the poem is the vehicle, the medium, in
which such collective thought takes place; it is governed by
no preceding principle except the capacity for thinking that
we all potentially share.

If we look at the three examples from Donne in "The
Metaphysical Poets," they exemplify Eliot's point that it
would be difficult to find "any precise use of metaphor,
simile, or other conceit" shared by all poems that fall under
that label (282). Donne's comparison of two lovers to a pair
of compasses in "A *Valediction*" (282) is compared favorably
to a figure of extended comparison in Cowley. This is contrasted to "a development by rapid association of thought
which requires considerable agility on the part of the reader"
in the second stanza of "A Valediction: Of Weeping." Eliot
does not provide the poem's title, and while he describes the
motion from globe to tear to deluge as "forced" by the poet,
he does not venture any further comment on what draws
the three images together. A third example from Donne is
then offered of a line that is made up of "brief words and
sudden contrasts: A *bracelet of bright hair about the bone*"
(283), though what is to be made of this sudden compound
remains unsaid. Eliot does not tell the reader what to make

of these conjunctions; indeed, he barely lets his reader
know what poem he is looking at. He offers no reading of a
poem, makes no attempt to unify it into a single structure.
It is not meaning at which he aims. Decontextualized, a
stanza, a line, even an allusion to a line is enough to set the
mind working at the properties of the image — of the objects
created by the imaginative conjunction created at the moment. These three examples are perhaps joined in the title
A *Valediction* that Eliot provides for "A Valediction: Forbidding Mourning." In these scenes of separation, of bidding
farewell, something remains of nothing, words that imagine
possibilities beyond, beside, outside the terms of ordinary
existence. It is certainly possible to regard these poems (and
many others in their traditions) as exercises in the ruses of
male power and privilege associated with Eliot's "mind of
Europe." Yet the new wholes being offered to contempla-
tion are also so decontextualized as to glimpse in their existence a thought world potentially other than the one in
which we might be reading Spinoza or sipping tea. Eliot
resists paraphrase, description of obvious subject matter or
theme, opening possibilities in the unsaid and inexistent.
Eliot avers about poetry what Giorgio Agamben suggests in
What Is Philosophy?: "What is at stake in philosophy is a
thing . . . that belongs neither to being nor to nonbeing"
(89).[33] Exploring "the poetic moment of thought," Agamben
asks what language does besides name things. What does
naming itself do? This is precisely the same question Aristotle answers in *De Anima* about what sensing or thinking
does in itself, as itself: each of these is itself in its activity.

Just as the citation from *The Revenger's Tragedy* in "Tradition and the Individual Talent" is capable of being read
as a metaphor for the poetic process as Eliot understood it,
so too can one take his citations from Donne. The lovers
as compasses turn flesh into metal; they have the hardness

of the objective correlative that radiates its suggestive aura. Bone and hair seem to work to join what has lived and died; what remains lifeless is yet attached to something separate from it that still seems alive, bright as an image. The central stanza of "A Valediction: Of Weeping" summons an image of the making of the image. The empty ball, a zero, becomes everything, "that, which was nothing, All," a new whole, a world. Poetic creation recreates the creation of the world recreated again between the lovers and the tear in which they dissolve, joined and separated. Here, as with "To His Coy Mistress," mortality, the limited life of any of us (indeed of our universe) is put into relation with what seems to be the unending force of a life that has no regard for our own, the life that goes on when ours has ended. Getting to the end first is as fast as we can go in Marvell's witty formulation of prevention of the end. The poem may be a place in which we can imaginatively live that life that is not our own. These questions are concerns in the other poems cited in "The Metaphysical Poets," Henry King's "The Exequy," and Lord Herbert of Cherbury's "Ode upon a Question Moved, Whether Love Should Continue For Ever." A citation from Chapman's *Revenge of Bussy d'Ambois* allows Eliot to phrase best the goal of thinking: "A man to join himself with th' Universe" (286). There is no self, no "rag of it as he" in this union of "One with that All." This new whole amalgamates and yet keeps separate One and All.

Homage to John Dryden

The third of Eliot's 1921 essays on seventeenth-century po-etry, "John Dryden," was occasioned by John Van Doren's study of the poet; Eliot's *TLS* review appeared on June 9, 1921, some months after "Andrew Marvell" and before "The Metaphysical Poets." Although Eliot would not "raise Mar-

vell to the level of Dryden or Milton," he happily granted
him greater approval, calling him a classic (302). That mixture of denigration and estimation clings too to Dryden and
Milton in "The Metaphysical Poets"; much as they are the
"two most powerful poets of the century" (288), they wielded
their influence, it seems, to no good: to them is owed the dissociation of sensibility, the separation of thought and feeling,
refined language for crude thoughts and emotions. It is thus
rather a surprise to find Eliot's essay on Dryden so full of
praise; it ends by recommending his work — not Laforgue —
as a model for modern poets. Opening his essay with a gesture similar to the others — noting the present inability to
enjoy Dryden's poetry — Eliot closes by imagining that "in
the next revolution of taste it is possible that poets may turn
to the study of Dryden" (316). "What is man to decide what
poetry is?" is the provocation to thought that Dryden raises
(315). Eliot resoundingly proclaims that whatever else one
might say about Dryden, he is certainly a poet; he makes the
commonplace and the prosaic poetry, the small and trivial,
large and magnificent: "Dryden is distinguished principally
for his *poetic* ability" (310). Eliot demonstrates this by noting
how Dryden enlarges and multiplies the genre in which he
most often worked, satire; it is not one thing, nor are his
dramas. "Wit," a subject of concern in the other two essays,
is widened to allow for the pure fun of Dryden, "surprise
after surprise of wit" (307) that seemed suspect in the essay
on Marvell for its lack of serious thought.

Whatever else Dryden's poems do, "they create the object
which they contemplate" (316), a condensed and precise
definition of what the poem is. As Marvell had been, Dryden
is declared "a successor of Jonson" and thereby "the ances-
tor of nearly all that is best in the poetry of the eighteenth
century" (305), but no comparison with Marvell is offered.
Rather, Eliot charts "the great advantage of Dryden over

Milton" (311), although, thanks to Dryden's "commonplace mind . . . his powers were . . . wider, but no greater, than Milton's" (314). Likewise, what he granted Dryden by way of Jonson he takes back: "Dryden lacked what his master Jonson possessed, a large and unique view of life; he lacked insight; he lacked profundity" (316). Nonetheless, Dryden may point the way forward for poetry, since "he remains one of those who have set standards for English verse which it is desperate to ignore" (316).

Perhaps the greatest surprise of "John Dryden," beyond the praises and diminishments Eliot delivers, is the fact that this is the only essay of the three that cites a poem in its entirety. Dryden's elegy on Oldham "deserves not to be mutilated" (315); "its lack of suggestiveness is compensated by the satisfying completeness of the statement" (316). That satisfaction is very much to Eliot's taste: the extravagant praise of the dead younger poet that occupies the first half of the poem is complicated by a consideration of what, had his life not been cut short, he might have accomplished. This double gesture of winning and losing has the suggestiveness Eliot denies the poem, since it puts us precisely on the frontier of the metaphysical questions that haunt the ontological status of the life of the poem. Borrowing the conceit of Ben Jonson's elegy about his first son, who bore his name, and whom Jonson calls his best piece of poetry, Dryden had begun to "think and call" Oldham "his own": Jonson's doubling of biological and poetic creation becomes another scene of affinity and filiation. Both poets are "cast in the same poetic mould," a cauldron that might recall the chemical vat. This sameness seems to cross the line between the living poet whose elegy we read and the poet he elegizes: Dryden's poetic model is not only Jonson's poem, it also is Milton's *Lycidas*. Explicitly, the model is Virgil, the race that Nisus and Euryalus ran, at first as a game, and then for real:

"Thus Nisus fell upon the slippery place,/Whilst his young
friend performed and won the race." In the *Aeneid*, Euryalus
and Nisus are lovers. The loser falls to let his lover win, then
the two fall together to be memorialized in the poem that
survives them. This scenario must remind us of the sulfuric
chamber in "Tradition and the Individual Talent," the meeting of "father" and "son," Brunetto Latini and Dante, in the
circle of the sodomites, the race lost and won there and recouped as the scene of poetic generation among the sodomites and loving couples (including Dante and Virgil) in
Purgatorio. The "unnatural" and supposedly ungenerative
meetings in such scenes suggest the origin and non/being
that is the life of the poem, "generous fruits, though gathered ere their prime" that still "show a quickness" perhaps
surpassing what the finish and polish of "maturing time"
would lend them: completion could rob them precisely of
the aura that permits them to go on.

Homage to John Dryden is the title of the 1924 volume
published by Virginia and Leonard Woolf's Hogarth Press,
which reprinted Eliot's 1921 essays on seventeenth-century
poetry. In the preface Eliot says nothing about the title, but
about an abandoned book project that would have surveyed
English poetry from Chapman and Donne to Dr. Johnson.
To do justice to this ambition "would have led me indirectly
into consideration of politics, education, and theology"
that he eschews, at least in this form, implicitly erecting a
frontier between poetics and politics. He leaves the essays
as they are, "cryptograms" for notions that, "if expressed directly, would be destined to immediate obloquy, followed
by perpetual oblivion." He perhaps means to forecast his
coming out in the preface to *For Lancelot Andrewes* as "classicist in literature, royalist in politics, and anglo-catholic in
religion."[34] The preface to that collection of essays promises

three books "in preparation": *The School of Donne, The Outline of Royalism,* and *The Principles of Modern Heresy* (x). Heading *Homage to John Dryden* with the Dryden essay may invite this decipherment of the cryptogram, although even his 1928 announcement is hedged in Eliot's usual manner, leaving open what he seems to have definitively shut down. The terms he uses, he notes, are vague, lacking definition, potentially "clap-trap." No inevitability leads the 1921 essays in the direction of the critical conservatism (to put Eliot's stance in the mildest terms) that followed.

In "For Lancelot Andrewes," Eliot compares Donne's preaching to Andrewes; the former is marked by his personality, while Andrewes "is wholly in his subject . . . wholly absorbed in the object" (29–30). Where earlier Eliot had managed to entertain the possibility of a relation between personality and impersonality, this dismissal of Donne had been anticipated in his Clark Lectures at Trinity College, Cambridge, in 1926.[35] The first of these continues to esteem Donne, but also moves him close to Dante. "One of the capital ideas of Donne, the one that is perhaps his peculiar gift to humanity, is that of the union, the fusion and identification of *souls* in sexual love," Eliot writes (54). In this, he continues, he is like Dante, who "always finds the sensuous equivalent, the physical embodiment, for the realisation of the most tenuous and refined intensity . . . of experience: it is as if the body were capable of maintaining life and consciousness" (57).

The five lectures that follow take it all back. Donne, we are told, separates flesh and spirit, does not fuse thinking and feeling; his is "a mind in chaos" (133), his conceits over-elaborate, unstructured, illogical; thought carried nowhere, merely for effect (as bad as Gertrude Stein, Eliot says [137]). Donne is a "voluptuary of thought," Crashaw a "voluptuary of religious emotion" (168), both deplorable. Marvell is no

metaphysical thinker. Jules Laforgue, hailed in 1921 as the
modern counterpart to the metaphysicals, is linked to them
in a modernity that is one of shards, dispersion, dissociations,
not merely of sensibility, but of the mind. Dante is now the
only poet capable of the kinds of poetic fusion Eliot once
saw as the ongoing project of poetry. To be a real metaphysical poet, one must believe in good and evil. One must be
a devout Christian. "For perfect art to arise, there must be a
kind of co-operation between philosophy and poetry" (222),
and there is exactly one example of it: Aquinas and Dante.
"Sensibility and intellect have been divided against each
other ever since the seventeenth century" (162). The dissociation is no longer blamed on Dryden and Milton; it was
there before them.

In 1931, Eliot once again rescinded his plans to publish
books justifying his rewriting and repudiation of his 1921 essays. In "Donne in Our Time," an essay written for a volume
celebrating the tercentenary of Donne's death, he claims
that Donne's time has passed, as has his youthful enthusiasm for him.[36] "By 1931 . . . there appears to me no possible
justification of turning my lectures into a book" (4). This was
true; by then other critics had developed and preserved the
1921 positions Eliot quickly had come to recant. Their rewriting of the canon would survive Eliot's undoings. Following
his hints, close readings of metaphysical poetry would become a leading method of criticism well into the twentieth
century. F. R. Leavis hails these developments in his 1936
collection of essays, *Revaluation*: "The work has been done,
the re-orientation effected: the heresies of ten years ago are
orthodoxy. Mr. Eliot's achievement is matter for academic
evaluation, his poetry is accepted, and his early observations
on the Metaphysicals and on Marvell provide currency for
university lectures and undergraduate exercises."[37] A phrase
from Eliot's essay on Marvell, "tough reasonableness,"

names Leavis's theme in his pursuit of a notion of the "life" that follows from literature.[38]

To the end of his career as a critic, Eliot was bent on repudiating these beginnings, most fully in "To Criticize the Critic," perhaps. There he hastens to deny the notion that he somehow created "the vogue for Donne" (21), while admitting how important Donne had been to him as a poet and crediting his poetry as the catalyst for interest in Donne. By 1961, the vehemence of his repudiations had faded: "Now . . . I turn more often the pages of Mallarmé than those of Laforgue, those of George Herbert, than those of Donne, of Shakespeare than of his contemporaries and epigoni" (23). Eliot's last piece of criticism on seventeenth-century poetry was a 1962 pamphlet on Herbert he contributed to the British Council series on "Writers and Their Work."[39] He stays within their biographical format (impersonality is no longer a term in his vocabulary); there are a few half-hearted gestures in the direction of the relation of intellect and sensibility in Herbert and Donne. While he resists the commonplace notion that Herbert is "the poet of a placid and comfortable easy piety" (14), Herbert nonetheless finally achieves "serenity" of belief (34).

Eliot's repudiations did not make their way into his *Selected Essays*, however. The 1921 essays are printed there unchanged; the volume opens with "Tradition and the Individual Talent." "Dante" is at its center but does not displace the non-Shakespearian authors that flank him: "John Marston" on one side, "The Metaphysical Poets" on the other. So, too, Eliot's poems cannot be caught in the critical designs he avowed. Hence, the words of the "you" initially called Brunetto Latini in *Little Gidding* (the poem's title summons up Herbert and Crashaw), are spoken on behalf of the Eliot Eliot was bent on repudiating: "I am not eager to rehearse / My thought and theory which you have forgotten" (II.58–59). In sustaining forgetting and remembering, Eliot remained engaged with the aporias of *De Anima* and of life-in-potential, which, as Agamben emphasizes, also means life impotent, the "constitutive co-belonging of potentiality and impotentiality," as he puts it in "What Is the Act of Creation?" (38). If poetry is "an operation in language that deactivates and renders inoperative its communicative and informative functions" (55), that suspension of the already given opens the way to the possible.

2

Anonymous Woolf

A Room of One's Own

"Had Shakespeare had a wonderfully gifted sister"

The figure of Shakespeare's sister that Virginia Woolf introduces in the third chapter of *A Room of One's Own* and conjures up again on its final page offers us a place to begin to consider her ontological and aesthetic concerns.[1] Judith Shakespeare focuses questions that arise on the first page of the book. There, Woolf puts to one side the relatively easy task that her subject — women and fiction — might demand, an account of some eighteenth- and nineteenth-century women writers of fiction.[2] She will give that account, but in the context of harder questions that do not resolve themselves in a roll call. What are women? What are the fictions, what the facts, about them? Women have virtually no history, no existence, according to books written about them by men whose only qualification to write on the topic is that they are men. In Judith Shakespeare, Woolf hypothesizes the existence of a woman who never existed to make appear what has otherwise been unknown and unacknowledged, possibilities and capacities that require fictional representation when the factual is a tissue of misrepresentations, the airing of prejudices and fears. If it was "impossible, completely and entirely, for any woman to have written the plays of Shakespeare in the age of Shakespeare" (46), as Woolf supposes on the basis of the research and reading she did, what would have happened if there had been a woman who mirrored Shakespeare in every respect except his gender?

Woolf imagines what her "story" would have been — failed accomplishment, forced pregnancy, suicide; that is how "the story would run," an existence tantamount to nonexistence. The supposition that Judith Shakespeare might have been the mirror of her brother falters at the start: "It is unthinkable that any woman in Shakespeare's day should have had Shakespeare's genius" (48). That is what all the historians aver, and the material conditions of women's lives seem to support it. Indeed, it is the premise of Woolf's book that without a certain amount of money in her purse and a room where she can shut the door and have the solitude and freedom to write, there can be no women writing. "Intellectual freedom depends upon material things" (106). That mind-body connection does not mean that impoverished, immobilized women cannot have the same kinds of minds as men have, however. "When, however, one reads of a witch being ducked, of a woman possessed by devils, of a wise woman selling herbs, or even of a very remarkable man who had a mother, then I think we are on the track of a lost novelist" (48). It is not, as she first thought, that women did not have the genius, the capacity; what they lacked was the possibility of making thought visible in writing. Their genius issued rather in scenes about women that are recorded (those that Woolf lists) and in the accomplishment of sons gifted with their mothers' intelligence and the prerogatives of male gender. So the story goes, but Woolf's mind, which never stops working, does not stop there. She ventures further "to guess that Anon, who wrote so many poems without signing them, was a woman" (49).[3]

With "Anon," the invisible and nonexistent woman now has a kind of name. It withdraws the proper name. It also refuses the boundary of true or false or perhaps crosses it into some other mode of categorization. As Woolf continues to aver that her story of Judith Shakespeare must be what happened to any woman in the sixteenth century who had literary talent — she would have taken her own life, since such a life was taken from her — she adds, "Her work would have gone unsigned" (49). Not unwritten, but unattached to a name that would alert the reader to the existence of a creature not supposed or acknowledged to have existed, a woman who made use of her own body to produce the work of her own mind. "Anonymity runs in their blood" (50), Woolf writes of the sixteenth-century woman to whom she has attached the name of literary genius: Shakespeare. "The truth is, I often like women" (109), Woolf further notes, almost in propria persona: "I like their anonymity" (110).

In liking anonymity, Woolf likes what remains to be seen and said, as is apparent in her writing in which she revises her thoughts on the pages we read; it may be embodied in women and fictions that will exist in a hundred years; it also exists now in the women she likes and who, like her, love other women. These women have never ceased to exist. "Now my belief is that this poet who never wrote a word and was buried at the crossroads still lives. She lives in you and me . . . for great poets never die; they are continuing presences" (112). In unrecorded lives, in unsigned poems, Woolf finds the life that continues.

It begins, her story about "a wonderfully gifted sister" (46), in her likeness to her brother. "She was as adventurous, as imaginative, as agog to see the world as he was. But she was not sent to school" (47). Because of her gender, she was shut in, self-taught (reading her brother's books sometimes), never encouraged by her parents. Like her brother she ran away (in her case, from the betrothal they insist upon), driven to fulfill her gift: "The birds that sang in the hedge were not more musical than she was. She had the quickest fancy, a gift like her brother's, for the tune of words. Like him, she had a taste for the theatre" (47). Taken in by a man who forces her into pregnancy, she ends by her own hand. Although Woolf's story is intent on the natural likeness of brother and sister, he has no part in her life or death. Similitudes join them. Likeness is not sameness, and the difference between them — what makes their relationship exist only in similitude — is their gender. What joins them is a talent, a gift, a capacity of mind.

Her gender, however, makes her "a very queer, composite being" (43); for centuries "women have served . . . as looking-glasses possessing the magic and delicious power of reflecting the figure of man at twice its natural size" (35). Demeaned to prop men up, women enact a Hegelian scene of denigration. These real-life scenes of female abnegation are answered by the women in fictions written by men. Shakespeare's women are among his greatest characters. How was that possible? "Doubtless Elizabethan literature would have been very different from what it was if the women's movement had begun in the sixteenth century and not in the nineteenth," Woolf avers (100). The war of the sexes based on insuperable difference is a modern invention, it seems; the "queer, composite being" that is woman describes the discrepant being of women seen in the difference between Shakespeare's women and the actual women of his time.

If one sought a historical solution to the quandary about

gender (for women in the sixteenth century did write about
their subjection), the theater might be the place to look.
Woolf's sister and brother resemble the supposed identical
twins Viola and Sebastian. The possibility of identity without difference for differently gendered characters lies in the
boy actors who played women's parts (and perhaps young
whiskerless men not yet fully adult). The Elizabethan stage
system seems to posit a third sex (Shakespeare's Rosalind
affirms the identification of boys and women) that gave
them the lability of cross-gendered performance. That likeness also produced same-gendered sexual situations. Woolf's
"queer, composite" woman she also calls "an odd monster"
(44), a word Viola uses in her soliloquy at the end of 2.2
in *Twelfth Night* about her assumption of the male attire
that provokes and impedes the desires that run between her,
Olivia, and the duke, cross-gender and same-sex desires at
once provoked by an object — how it looks, what it hides that
is nonetheless seen. The solution to these dilemmas in the
transferability of desire is embodied in Viola and Sebastian
as identical twins.

Woolf approaches this identity in her story by describing it as a gift, a talent, a shared mental disposition. This
state of mind is also described with the same word she uses
for Shakespearean embodiment: androgyny. Close to the
end of *A Room of One's Own*, Woolf inscribes what should
have been the first sentence in "Women and Fiction": "It
is fatal for any one who writes to think of their sex. It is fatal to be a man or woman, pure or simple; one must be
woman-manly or man-womanly" (102–3). Fatal to think of
oneself as one sex: Woolf encourages one to live in a thought
that may name the originary state of the mind: represented
by brother and sister imagined in their imaginary similitude.
From what we know of his life, "we know nothing about
Shakespeare's mind"; we know his mind from his writing. "If

ever a mind was incandescent, unimpeded, . . . it was Shakespeare's mind" (56). "The androgynous mind . . . is naturally
creative, incandescent and undivided. In fact, one goes back
to Shakespeare's mind as the type of the androgynous, of the
man-womanly mind, though it would be impossible to say
what Shakespeare thought of women" (97). "Shakespeare's
mind" is not identical to "Shakespeare" in this sentence; the
former figures the anonymous creative mind. "Shakespeare's
sister," too, is a figure, a simile for this identity. Indeed, figuratively speaking, Shakespeare has another sister in Woolf's
text, Jane Austen, and yet another — in Woolf.

"We do not know Jane Austen and we do not know Shakespeare, and for that reason Jane Austen pervades every word
that she wrote, and so does Shakespeare." The two are not
identical twins except insofar as "the minds of both had consumed all impediments" (67). In Austen's case, these are the
impediments of her gender, the exclusions, refusals that mar
the writing of all other women — even the genius Charlotte
Brontë, railing angrily against her confinement, or George
Eliot, writing under a male name, living "in sin" seques-
tered. If the earliest writing of English women is unsigned,
anonymous, the writing of those who managed to consume
the impediments of biographical existence (limits of gender,
class, education, capital) achieve the anonymity of an authorial name. Austen invented a new sentence.

"Attached to life at all four corners"

Woolf's list of androgynous male writers, headed by Shakespeare, ends with Proust, "wholly androgynous, if not perhaps a little too much of a woman" (102). Woolf signals a
third-sex explanation of male homosexuality and perhaps
alludes to the opening lines of Shakespeare's sonnet 20, "A
Womans face with natures owne hand painted/Hast thou

the Master Mistris of my passion." As the contemporary woman writer who would be Shakespeare's sister, Woolf imagines Mary Carmichael; her novel, *Life's Adventure*, features a couple, Chloe and Olivia: "Chloe liked Olivia . . ." (80) is all we read from this fictional fiction. "Sometimes women do like women" (81), as did Shakespeare's Olivia (as did Woolf, as *Orlando* makes apparent). "Like" is key here; "like" sometimes means liking someone alike. "Mary Carmichael," the novelist of the future, is a possible name for the anonymous "I" of *A Room of One's Own*. "Call me Mary Beton, Mary Seton, Mary Carmichael or by any name you please" (5). These names can be found in an anonymous ballad extant in various recensions. Woolf joins her authorial anonymity to the anonymity of the tradition of women writers. "Life's adventures," which titles the novel Mary Carmichael has written, runs from anonymity to anonymity. Through that route one enters "that vast chamber where nobody has yet been" to find "words that are hardly syllabled yet" (83), "some entirely new combination" that will "absorb the new into the old without disturbing the intricate and elaborate balance of the whole" (84). Olivia and Chloe work together in a laboratory; one of them is married and has children, the other is single. The entirely new combination of words is figured as a relation between women.

The trick of Mary Carmichael's existence is that "she wrote as a woman, but as a woman who has forgotten that she is a woman" (91). Woolf preserves the category of "woman" even as she separates it from the word "woman" that defines a site of prohibition, incapacity, and inability. To be what she is she must forget what she is said to be; the same word rewritten is unwritten, same and different at once. Women remain women, but what they are remains to be seen. Shakespeare's plays "seem to hang there complete by themselves"; the condition of the work of art appears to be its detachment from the hand that made it, whole and complete in itself. But "fiction is like a spider's web, attached ever so lightly perhaps, but still attached to life at all four corners" (41). The spider, according to the myths about Arachne, defied the gods. Aphra Behn, for Woolf, is the first writer with whom "begins the freedom of mind" (63) that Shakespeare enjoyed and Jane Austen found as well. She earned a living from writing and lived a sexually free life: "All women together ought to let flowers fall upon the tomb of Aphra Behn" (65). The detachment of the work depends upon such embodied material achievements.

Judith Shakespeare, Woolf's imaginary sister, was the name of the actual sister of Shakespeare's son Hamnet. Fraternal twins: he died young but lent his name to Hamlet; she lived on for many years. Woolf's imagined sister is "a very queer composite being." In her story, her brother survived her death; the real brother did that as the character his father created as his namesake.[4] Woolf's story has other similar literary attachments. After the fictional Judith's suicide, this question is asked: "Who shall measure the heat and violence of the poet's heart when caught and tangled in a woman's body?" (48) It draws on lines York speaks to Queen Margaret in 3 *Henry VI* before she kills him: "O tiger's heart wrapped in a woman's hide" (1.4.137). York calls this Amazon a ravening animal disguised as a woman, a figure that does not settle into neat binarisms, since her woman's skin is animal hide. Nick Greene, the man who impregnated Woolf's Judith, renames Robert Greene. In *Greene's Groatsworth of Wit*, he calls Shakespeare "an upstart Crow, beautified with our feathers, that with his *Tygers hart wrapt in a Players hyde*, supposes he is as well able to blast out a blanke verse as the best of you: and being an absolute *Iohannes fac totum*, is in his own conceit the only Shake-scene in a country."[5] Shakespeare, the actor pretending to be an author, is put into the position of the actor boying the woman. Woolf's rewriting recalls both a woman Shakespeare created and the woman his detractor and rival would make him into.

"The mind is certainly a very mysterious organ," Woolf comments toward the end of *A Room of One's Own*; composed of "severances and oppositions," it has "no single being" (96). There are "two sexes in the mind" as there are of the body; everyone is a product of the degree and nature of their "fusion." Working together, the mind regains its "natural fusion" and achieves its unity through combination. "A great mind is androgynous. It is when this fusion takes place that the mind is fully fertilized and uses all its faculties" (97). It creates what may be in what is.

Art has "a certain looking-glass likeness to life" (70). "Life conflicts with something not life"; by working through impasses of what is and what is said to be, "something called integrity" emerges, a book that holds life and "not life" together. Readers know a novel is true to life when it provokes this response: "But this is what I have always felt and known and desired!" (71). Our minds become as incandescent as the writer's is when it has consumed its anger at the "not life" that life offers and finds the life that is. Perhaps, Woolf speculates, "Nature, in her most irrational mood, has traced in invisible ink on the walls of the mind a premonition which these great artists confirm; a sketch which only needs to be held to the fire of genius to become visible" (71). Written in invisible ink, this is the writing of Anon that we all are and that we know when our minds are aglow, burning.

With it comes the "freedom to think of things in themselves" (39). There is "a force in things" that drives us together just as there is "the unity of the mind" (95). "Reality" names that realization. The writer "has the chance to live more than other people in the presence of this reality" (108) and to convey it in invisible ink, new sentences, unsyllabled

words drawing us into unvisited rooms of our own that are
not just ours. "Think of things in themselves" (109). "Our
relation is to the world of reality and not only to the world of
men and women" (112). Both worlds exist, but "the common
life . . . is the real life and not the little separate lives we
live as individuals" (112). The common life, the life that the
common readers lives, is this anonymous life.

The Common Reader

On the final page of *A Room of One's Own*, "common" describes the life to be lived "if we live another century or so"
when we might "see humans not always in their relation
to each other but in relation to reality." Woolf further explains the nature and reach of this relation; it is like "the
sky, too, and the trees or whatever it may be in themselves"
(112). What we are in ourselves is what trees and sky are:
things that exist. The in-itselfness of anything is not only
what makes each unique, but also what we have in common. In-itselfness has no name; it is not treeness or skyness
or humanity; it is what joins them and us in and to existence.

"Common" names the reader in the volumes of her essays Woolf gathered as *The Common Reader* in 1925 and in
The Second Common Reader in 1932.[6] With the exception
of an essay on Russian fiction, another on the Greeks, and a
third on Montaigne (all in the first volume, the first two ap-
pearing there for the first time), the essays concern English
literature, arranged roughly chronologically, but not consti-
tuting anything like the standard canon. There is no essay
on Spenser, Shakespeare, or Milton, for example; there are
essays on Austen, *Jane Eyre*, and *Wuthering Heights*, but
none on Dickens. Woolf combines brief pieces on memoirs,
biographies of or by a variety of authors, eyeing the plight of
women, often written by them, trapped by the limitations

of gender imposed on them, yet sometimes managing to write themselves some way out of their situation, if not into canonicity; also scanned are aristocratic women of means "confined . . . to a bird-cage" (197) and men, venerated for their learning, who kill the materials they mean to bring to life and make available to those of us less learned (Bentley on *Paradise Lost* is Exhibit A). The field of writing is leveled, democratized; these disparate texts share something that any reader (Woolf includes herself in this category) can find in any of them.

Woolf joins her common readers to books that might be thought common in pejorative, class-, or sexually inflected ways (books for people with "common" intelligence; "common" women as in *The Revenger's Tragedy* of whom it is said that "'Tis common to be common" [sexually profligate; 3.5.38]). These and the broader sociopolitical double of the "common" of the "commonwealth" and the House of Commons, for example, resonate with Woolf's formulations of the relationship between people and things in themselves. What we have in common, moreover, is the fact that we all die and yet that our bounded lives coexist with and in a life that continues beyond our own; trees and sky seem the same, yet the sky changes at every moment, trees die; yet these are part of a life that seems inextinguishable (the end of the universe is unimaginably far off). We can sometimes experience that life in this one, with others, in books that live longer than we do.

We do this thanks to our intellectual and affective capacities. The sacralizing term "canon" could suggest that only certain books usher us into such experiences. Woolf's project in *The Common Reader* volumes refuses that supposition along with the notion that only certain readers have the capacity for it. Woolf educes a capacity that all readers have, an aesthetic education that brings out what is already in us. Her

reading of the literature of the past points ahead. Each volume ends with an essay on the conditions of contemporaneity that may yet find possibilities in the past. "How It Strikes
a Contemporary," the final essay in the first volume, notes
that modern writers are intent "to give expression to the differences which separate them from the past and not to the
resemblances which connect them to it" (237), a presentism
that Woolf links to a concern with the "self, in short." "To
believe that your impressions hold good for others," Woolf
enjoins, "is to be released from the cramp and confinement
of personality" (238). She urges critics to "take a wider, a less
personal view of modern literature, and look indeed upon
the writers as if they were engaged in some vast building,
which being built by common effort, the separate workmen
may well remain anonymous" (240).

The Common Reader opens with a page with that title and
with a citation from a critic not usually noted for such impersonal qualities: Samuel Johnson. Woolf quotes from the
last paragraph of his "Life of Gray": "I rejoice to concur with
the common reader; for by the common sense of readers,
uncorrupted by literary prejudices, after all the retirements
of subtilty and the dogmatism of learning, must be finally
decided all claims to poetical honours." Johnson finally
hands over his exercises of judgment to join the common
reader, concluding an essay whose measured praise of Gray
is followed by an evaluation of his poetry that he hopes will
not "be looked on as an enemy to his name, if I confess that
I contemplate it with less pleasure than his life."[7] Exacting,
scathing comments follow, alleviated by his happy concur-
rence at the end with the common estimation of Gray's "Elegy Written in a Country Churchyard." Gertrude's reminder
to Hamlet — "'Tis common: all that lives must die" — also is
Gray's subject. Johnson bows to the common reader he de-

scribes as "worse educated, . . . not gifted . . . so generously"
as the scholar-critic in recognition of the figure in Gray's
poem, the "mute inglorious Milton" that Woolf rewrites in
A Room of One's Own as "some mute and inglorious Jane
Austen" (48). Her other name is Anon.

Johnson links the common reader to common sense, a
term that tends now to mean a rough and ready empiricist
recognition of something so immediately obvious (so ideo-
logically inscribed) as to require no thought. Philosophi-
cally, "common sense" has a long history going back at least
to Plato and Aristotle, who variously suppose something un-
derlying all thinking and feeling that marks our metaphysical attachment to what is. Common sense also can suppose
a shared capacity for sense that exceeds and joins together
the particular capacities of any organ. Woolf's parsing of
Johnson's sentence glances in all these directions. Common
sense is an "instinct to create for himself, out of whatever
odds and ends he can, some kind of whole"; this whole cannot last but affords "temporary satisfaction" even if what it
grabs hold of is superficially related. In this exercise, something happens in what might appear to be futile thought, the
opportunity of something close enough to "the real object to
allow of affection, laughter, and argument." Common sense
is an exercise of our creative faculty; however mistakenly it
may be by the lights of knowledge and expertise, it opens
the possibility of the near miss that is also a near hit on some
truth otherwise unavailable, inarticulate, as yet unsyllabled.
We will know it when we like it, enjoy it, want to argue it further. "The common reader . . . reads for his own pleasure,"
but his own is not just that. As Johnson says about Gray's
"Elegy," it holds up "a mirrour in every mind," "sentiments
to which every bosom returns an echo." Reading the poem,
its most original lines persuade the reader to think they con-
tain what "he has always felt" (2:264), Johnson writes, the

experience Woolf inscribes in *A Room of One's Own*: "But this is what I have always felt and known and desired" (71).

"This quickening, this enchantment . . ."

The three essays that open *The Common Reader* were written specifically for the volume. Only the third — on Hakluyt's *Voyages* — explicitly engages an early modern English text. The first concerns Chaucer, the author Dryden called the father of English poetry, the second, classical Greek texts.[8] Woolf breaks sequential literary history. She asks what modernity can make (did make) of these pasts. "The Pastons and Chaucer" answers by finding commonality between Chaucer and letters not in the literary canon (is Hakluyt?). Woolf focuses on those written by Margery Paston. She acted as bailiff for her husband's estate in his absence; after his death she enjoined his son and heir to build a monument to his deceased father. Margery sought to assure the patriarchy; the wayward young man had no such interest, nor in the life after death a monument supposes. In him, Woolf finds the advent of a modernity that also was Chaucer's. "Chaucer fixed his eyes upon the road before him, not upon the world to come" (16). So doing, he "made a complete model of the world" (17). The young Sir John, of an "indolent and luxurious temperament," (9) also lives in the present; he buys "clocks and trinkets" (10); he "likes to read." "He would sit reading Chaucer, wasting his time, dreaming," finding his life in what he read: "the very skies, fields, and people he knew, but rounded and complete." Out on business, he would recall "some description or saying that bore upon the present moment and fixed it, some string of words would charm him, and putting aside the pressure of the moment he would hasten home to sit in his chair and learn the end of the story" (11).

Reading relieves the moment of its pressure: ordinary temporal distinctions glide; oppositions between this world and the next, between generations and genders, lose their demarcations. So, too, the language of daily, ordinary, common business that fills Margery's letters, is occasionally enlivened "into some shrewd saw or solemn curse." Hers is the language that Chaucer "must have heard" (22). Woolf hears his language in words written long after Chaucer died. "To learn the story — Chaucer can still make us wish to do that" (11), Woolf puts herself where she left Sir John, charmed by Chaucer, his language, "matter of fact, unmetaphorical, . . . fitted for narrative" (22). "Chaucer, it seems, has some art by which the most ordinary words and the simplest feelings when laid side by side make each other shine; when separated lose their lustre." "All these common things" (19), arranged in poetic wholes, recreate our pleasure in the world we see. Chaucer's world actually reflected an openness and expansiveness no longer ours; he speaks more frankly and directly about aspects of bodily existence that now seem out of bounds except in obliquity or obscenity. The father of poetry does this especially well in his portraits of frank and fresh young women, each entirely graspable as herself, and yet each like the other in being "content to be herself" (14). Likewise the Wife of Bath: "The sound of that old woman's voice is still" (15), an unrecoverable voice of a past stilled in the past, yet still resonating.

"We know that though this world resembles, it is not in fact our daily world. It is the world of poetry" in which everything occurs more intensely and compactly within some immediate, momentary order that seems more than that; in Chaucer's use of language it is "as if we read our thoughts before words cumbered them," so much so that "this quickening, this enchantment, we cannot prove . . . by quotation" (19). This common language exists in our minds; it is not

exactly there on the page, but rather in the relationship between what we see in the real world, what we read written
on the page, and the mirror in our mind that recomposes
these realities into one more lasting, grasped in moments
whose intensity is measured by our absorption in them, as
we waste our time in another temporality. "We are left to
stray and stare and make out a meaning for ourselves" (18) in
"all these common things" (19). Reading Chaucer with the
Paston letters, Woolf ushers us into an understanding of our
common experience as readers.

In "On Not Knowing Greek," our commonality resides
in two conditions we all share: "our ignorance" of Greek
coupled with something "all the more strange," "that we
should wish to know Greek, try to know Greek, feel for ever
drawn back to Greek, and be for ever making up some notion of the meaning of Greek" (23). Not knowing applies
to the "unlearned" who read classic texts in translation and
depend upon the learned assurance that Greek "is the literature of masterpieces" (37). It applies to the learned, Woolf
included: she quotes Greek; she notes the inadequacy of
translations, their antiquated diction or prolixity. She knows
Greek well enough to know that it can't be translated. If so,
she knows it only to know that we really don't, gaining the
knowledge that Socrates promulgated when, in Plato, he in-
terrogated some "handsome boy" spouting received notions,
demanding that he arrive at the truth — invariably, that the
lad didn't know what he was saying. "What matters is not so
much the end we reach as our manner of reaching it. . . . It
is to enjoy the greatest felicity of which we are capable" (32),
seduced into thinking.

Not knowing Greek can never stop us from the desire to
know. When we start to read an ancient text, Woolf writes,
"at once the mind begins to fashion itself surroundings"; we

imagine the world in which the text was produced and its resemblance to a country village we may know where, it seems, nothing has changed, a "little community," a "common stock," where "life has cut the same grooves for centuries" (24). Is there such a world anywhere? Has there ever been one?

In its unfathomable imaginative, creative capacity, the mind Woolf imagines is ours in common — is an "out-of-door" world. We hear the voices of performers in an amphitheater playing parts so old and so well-known they seem immemorial. Their availability makes for a difficulty. They speak a kind of shorthand; "It is not so easy for us to decide what gives these cries of Electra in her anguish their power to cut and wound and excite" (26). The problem with Sophocles's heroine (it is not hers alone) is that she appears almost to be lacking character, the nuances of particularity that a modern author would give us to make her knowable (Proust is Woolf's example). It is not just characters who, despite being so well-known, are so inscrutable; it is the authors who created them. "Greek is the impersonal literature" (23), Woolf announces at the opening and reiterates at the end of her essay. In that anonymous in-itselfness — in its being — it excites us to the prospect of an ultimate knowledge: "It is this that draws us back and back to the Greeks," Woolf reiterates, "the stable, the permanent, the original human being to be found there" (27).

The characters in Greek tragedy are originals but also not recognizably human; they are "heroism itself, . . . fidelity itself" (27); we are not types but ourselves. And yet, Woolf continues, because they exemplify "the way everybody has always behaved . . . we understand them more easily and more directly than we understand the characters in *The Canterbury Tales*. These are the originals, Chaucer's the varieties of the human species" (27). Woolf began her essay

suggesting "a tremendous breach in tradition" between us
and the Greeks, noting too the "chasm" in the few hundred
years that separate "our" English ancestors, Chaucer and the
Pastons, from Plato, Plato from "the vast tide of European
chatter" (23).

Woolf entertains the supposition that in Greek tragedy,
the "undifferentiated voices" of the chorus (29) might, collectively, be ours, and might mediate between us and the remote characters enacting passions that "remain, something
that has been stated and must eternally endure" (28). But
that is not what the chorus does. In Sophocles, the chorus
dwells unaccountably on some detail from which "a general
force, a symbolic power" (31) is rendered; the chorus in Eu-
ripides "speaks darkly" (30), posing "incongruities" (31) in
a language and syntax more suited to the page that can be
pondered than in speech heard to be taken in immediately
or not at all. Aeschylus has his chorus speak metaphorically.
"To understand him it is not so necessary to understand
Greek as to understand poetry" (30). The "blast of meaning"
in his words lies in their making the connections of "a rapid
flight of mind"; we grasp it instinctively. "We cannot know
exactly what it means" (30).

Metaphor in Aeschylus shows us "not the thing itself but
the reverberations and reflection which, taken into the mind,
the thing has made; close enough to the original to illustrate
it, remote enough to heighten, enlarge, and make splendid"
(31). The opacities of the chorus put in question how we
ever get from a particular to the general, from an original
to a copy, how unrelated things nonetheless combine into
new wholes. Greek is an ungraspable totality that cannot be
broken apart. Our world fell apart sometime in the opening
years of the twentieth century, perhaps before the war, certainly after it. That break reiterates the earlier one between
Plato and Europe; it is a gap like the one between "the thing

itself" and what the mind makes of it. "Back and back we are drawn" over and again "to steep ourselves in what, perhaps, is only an image of the reality, not the reality itself" (35). We are drawn to imagine a life of the mind that is part of "the art of living" (33) as exemplified in *The Symposium* (with its heady discussions combined with relaxed drinking and flirtation) or in *The Odyssey*, where "actions seem laden with beauty" because the characters who perform them are so unselfconscious (38). Like their authors their "unconsciousness . . . means that the consciousness is stimulated to the highest extent" (37); their unconsciousness is ours: knowing and unknowing coincide in the fullness of the life we attempt to live. "It is not to the cloistered disciplinarian mortifying himself in solitude that we are to turn" (33); rather, "it is to the Greeks that we turn when we are sick of the vagueness, of the confusion, of the Christianity and its consolations, of our own age" (38).

It is not only to the Greeks that we turn for this experience. The words that Austen's Emma speaks, "I will dance with you," bear "the whole weight of the book." Her "figures are bound and restricted to a few definite movements," as are the Greeks'. Shakespeare appears in "On Not Knowing Greek," beside Aeschylus; his "meaning is just on the far side of language . . . the meaning which in moments of astonishing excitement and stress we perceive in our minds without words." Dostoevsky attempts to go there, too, pointing, but not arriving at the "meaning Shakespeare succeeds in snaring" (31). Words for wordless meaning: this is what it is not to know Greek.

With "The Elizabethan Lumber Room," Woolf begins a consideration of early modern literature.[9] It extends through two previously published essays, "Notes on an Elizabethan

Play" and "Montaigne," to another piece written for *The Common Reader*, "The Duchess of Newcastle."[10] The "lumber room" in the title of the initial essay refers first to the books themselves, the "magnificent volumes" that Richard Hakluyt began gathering late in the sixteenth century, narratives of the "voyages, traffics, and discoveries" of the English in the sixteenth century, earlier documents related to them, lists of cargoes of goods traded, information about participants in these ventures. These books, rarely "read through," Woolf observes, are more like "a great bundle of commodities . . . , an emporium, a lumber room strewn with ancient sacks, obsolete nautical instruments, huge bales of wool, and little bags of rubies and emeralds." We ransack them over and again, "for ever" making our own discoveries as we sniff "the strange smells of silks and leathers and ambergris" (39).

Woolf treats the books as if they were the things they name, as if their words had the textures, odors, feel of the objects named in them. So doing, she animates the volumes, filling them with the life that she perceives in them, a life perhaps coincident with whatever it was that led Hakluyt to gather them in the first place. She rebundles these items, drawing together disparate pieces that Hakluyt barely ordered in the hodgepodge of his ever-expanding enterprise. Woolf no more orders it than he did, if by ordering we mean providing some explicit logic for her encounters with this treasure trove. Instead, she dips in here and there, pulls out a well-known name, Sir Humphrey Gilbert, for instance, attached to the Roanoke colony, or well-known stories. Without mentioning Frobisher, she recounts how he brought two native Americans back to England from his northwest passage journey; sketchier mentions of sailors lost at sea or returning unrecognizable to England are not so easily traced.

In this essay and those that follow, Woolf proves herself a paradigmatic common reader, "guided by an instinct to create for himself out of whatever odds and ends he can come by, some kind of whole," as she put it in the opening piece titled "The Common Reader," "a portrait of a man, a sketch of an age, a theory of the art of writing" (1). By the end of "The Elizabethan Lumber Room," Hakluyt's volumes have led her to Montaigne and Sir Philip Sidney, Ben Jonson, Robert Greene, and Sir Thomas Browne. Voyages into the unknown, "the amazing new world" (42) unaccountably, and yet through their extravagance, provide "the new words, the new ideas, the waves, the savages, the adventures" that constitute early modernity; they will lead Woolf to exemplify the period with two essay portraits — of Montaigne and Margaret Cavendish — and to address herself to a theory of writing that pushes against suppositions of her contemporary novelists and their readers. Against them she marshals the group she calls by the shorthand term "Elizabethans" (her focus on drama is Jacobean, a composite of Ford, Chapman, Webster); Montaigne's French essays (Woolf quotes from about twenty), and the "poems . . . plays . . . philosophies . . . orations . . . discourses" of Cavendish that "moulder in the gloom of public libraries" (69). Woolf excavates what still lives in them: "The vast bulk of the Duchess is leavened by a vein of authentic fire" (77).

"Odds and ends of priceless value and complete worthlessness"

Woolf sums up Hakluyt in these words at the opening of "The Elizabethan Lumber Room" (39). The combination of valuelessness and the invaluable describes the nexus of the reading project of *The Common Reader* and the questions it raises about what literature is, what it does, how it works. As material objects, books have minimal value; yet from these almost nothings something comes: not just books about them or derived from them, but something transmitted to readers, not in predictable ways, not in any pattern that can be rationalized or foreseen, yet that can be recognized as common if not necessarily to be explained by some singular theory. The method of the common reader is no method at all: a response occurs; it may be recorded in an essay; it may well be revised, even contradicted, even as it is being written. So doing, it aims at a truth, a reality, at a "life" graspable in the momentary wonder of its grasping. How is it that the "gulf" is crossed from the Pastons to "Elizabethan Court ladies . . . reading histories, or 'writing volumes of their own, or translating of other men's into our English and Latin tongue,' while the younger ladies played the lute and the citharne"? What are the "springs" of "the characteristic Elizabethan exuberance" (42–43) if not Hakluyt's unpromising, yet tantalizing lumber rooms, or, for that matter, the new wholes in Woolf's revelatory transformations of "Elizabethan" authorship?

"The whole of Elizabethan literature," Woolf writes, is "strewn with gold and silver; with talk of Guiana's rarities, and references to that America . . . which was not merely a land on a map, but symbolised the unknown territories of the soul" (43). Her claim immediately prompts the name "Montaigne," and just as immediately a comparison to Sir Philip Sidney; Woolf quotes from *The Defense of Poesie*, Sidney describing the poet's arrival with a tale and a tune, promising childhood enchantments; she cuts off the citation after some twenty lines, noting that it runs "for seventy-six words more" (44). For all his attempts to present the poet as a harmless charmer capable of magical transports, Sidney "is never quick, never colloquial": his assumption of the voice speaking to and as a common reader is a ploy, an artifice; it is not alive despite its "sudden flashes of felicity and splendid phrases." The lure that Sidney claims as the aim of the poet catches us unawares and tricks us into acting properly. "Unable to grasp a thought closely and firmly, or to adapt itself flexibly and exactly to the chops and changes of the mind," (44) Sidney circumlocutes around a foregone conclusion rather than opening possibilities of ongoing thought that might lead one to know how to live. Sidney seems an age behind Montaigne to Woolf; he also has the "freshness and audacity" of youth; he is capable of "freely" reaching "his hand for a metaphor." The journey to the "America" offered by Hakluyt can be found in Sidney, too. Woolf makes him "quick," alive again, after decrying his ploys.

So too with Hakluyt; his texts could be instruments of imperialism (Woolf quotes Froude as she begins to describe the voyages of discovery), the "decoying" of young men into the service of empire and profiteering advertised as good for the nation. Her indulgence in his "fine stories," like the one about a merchant who made his way to Moscow and saw the Emperor seated on a throne of gold could lead in that direction, but not when the treasure turns into an object of aesthetic appreciation; it carries another meaning: "The sight upon which the English merchant first set eyes has the brilliancy of a Roman vase dug up and stood for a moment in the sun, until, exposed to the air . . . it dulls and crumbles away" (41). Momentary wonder and beauty quickly fade along with the false lure of eternal empires. A page later, Woolf wonders how such visions led to Elizabethan culture and recalls Montaigne, who, "over the water," across the channel, "brooded in fascination upon savages, cannibals, society, and government" (43), concluding his thinking about "the greatness of Empire, . . . the moral duty of civilising the savage" with the injunction she phrases in her essay on Montaigne this way: "But look at the Spanish in Mexico, cried Montaigne in a burst of rage" (60).

How is it that "the Elizabethan view of reality," filled with stories that reveal a history of exploitation, can still be used to expand our souls and our grasp of reality? In "Notes on an Elizabethan Play," Woolf probes this question by way of a scene from *Bussy d'Ambois* in which an "angry unicorn" in Armenia attacks and kills a jeweler who hoped to steal "the treasure of his brow" (49). What kind of reality is this? The real we know is bound by "life and death," economic and social positions. There are no unicorns. Fantastical Elizabethan worlds offer "the relief of being free to wander," although they do not sustain that promise. Soon enough, the excesses of ranting, of plot extremity, of murders upon murders, of exhausting ruses of cross-dressing plots, of madness, prove wearisome.[11] "We know indeed that . . . reality is a chameleon quality" (50); to see life whole we must set our sights somewhat higher than the absolutely banal and mundane. Ultimately, the Elizabethans "bore us because they suffocate our imaginations rather than set them to work" (50). And yet these excessive plays touched something in their large and diverse audiences that we share with them, as they do with ancient Greeks who gathered in the open-air amphitheaters to see tragedies that do not show people as we think we know them; so, too, "there are no characters in Elizabethan drama, only violences" (51). Annabella in *'Tis Pity She's a Whore* is not someone with coherent thought processes, but "a series of tremendous vicissitudes," and yet relentlessly the same.

To complain about her character is however to miss the point; she embodies a kind of intensity that the novel cannot deliver. Anna Karenina could never tell Vronsky what the heroine of *The White Devil* says: "You have oft for these two lips / Neglected cassia or the natural sweets / Of the spring-violet." "The extremes of passion are not for the novelist; the perfect marriages of sense and sound are not for him" (53). Ford's Annabella is not in love, she is love. The imaginative reconstructions of the new world, from Hakluyt to the Elizabethan/Jacobean stage, draws on "the inexhaustible richness of human sensibility" (54). Woolf's metaphor turns real exploitation into imaginary literary gold. Language fails here, as Woolf had noted elsewhere it is bound to do when it tries to reach where the mind goes beyond what can be said or has been done. "The mind is so saturated with sensibility" that we must still await a literature capable of releasing "the enormous burden of the unexpressed" (54). From Hakluyt's metaphorical lumber room Woolf traces a theoretical route to the literature of the future, forbidding the "ruling off of one form of literature or decreeing its inferiority to others." The literature of the past reads us differently; it "splits us into two parts as we read" (48). From these divisions, new wholes arise. "Wandering in the maze of the impossible and the tedious story suddenly some passionate intensity seizes us; some sublimity exalts, or some melodious song enchants" (57). "So we ramble through the jungle, forest, and wilderness of Elizabethan drama" (56), not trapped as we experience "tedium and delight, pleasure and curiosity" (57), nor fully satisfied either as our reading negotiates both sides of the split between then and now all at once.

Split . . . into two parts as we read

Woolf's journey outward to new terrains leads inward to domains of the soul. Past and present split and suture inner and outer. Ending her "Notes on an Elizabethan Play," Woolf yearns for solitude; "The Elizabethan Lumber Room" follows a similarly double trajectory: "The stage was necessary and the growth of self-consciousness," she writes (45). Jonson's *Silent Woman* illustrates this dialogue: the outward other-facing "publicity of the stage" created what Sidney's "uninterrupted monologue" failed to achieve: commonality

with another. Nonetheless, if "the publicity of the stage and
the perpetual presence of a second person were hostile to
the growing consciousness of one's self," self-consciousness
necessarily doubles itself to be aware of itself. "Brooding in
solitude over the mysteries of the soul," one separates oneself
from oneself. The soul remains a mystery, self-consciousness
an endless journey into an unknowable terrain. From Hakluyt, Woolf turns to Sir Thomas Browne.

The title of his best-known book, *Religio Medici*, con-
cisely names the divided and doubled worlds of science and
belief that he straddles. His portrait of himself Woolf happily
allows to be that of a "character" in the most colloquial sense
of the term, a bundle of habits and eccentricities that are his
alone, yet they are not separate from the weird science lore
he accepts or the demand of his faith that he believe the impossible. Browne loves to lose himself in an "*O altitudo!*" —
the Latin word means both height and depth; the doctor
feels his patient's pulse yet cannot affirm he lives. Browne's
self-explorations resemble the discoveries and vagaries of
Hakluyt. He is the globe he explores, "the astonishing vis-
tas that open before his imagination. 'We carry with us the
wonders we seek without us; there is all Africa and her prod-
igies in us'" (46). The new world, a projection of the other
world within, is made by our minds; it could be that we sleep
through a life of waking dreams.

Sir Thomas Browne is produced by his writing; he lives
there not behind the sober face of the doctor at his patient's
bedside nor in the obsessive vagaries of the scientist sure
that by finding quincunxes everywhere he will discover the
principle of life. "Now we are in the presence of sublime
imagination; now rambling through one of the finest lumber rooms in the world — a chamber stuffed from floor to
ceiling with ivory, old iron, broken pots, urns, unicorns'
horns and magic glasses full of emerald lights and blue mys-

tery" (47). As readers we are with Sir Thomas Browne in early modernity and, at the same time, in "our private life" (45) in these encounters on the page whose "life" joins both now and then, him and us.

For Montaigne, the life of the soul is at odds with colonialist, imperial ventures as well as the wars of religious belief tearing Europe apart. "The soul, or life within us, by no means agrees with the life outside us. If one has the courage to ask her what she thinks, she is always saying the very opposite to what other people say" (60). "She" is our soul, *âme* in French, *anima* in Latin. "O my America! new-found-land," Woolf quotes Donne, imagining he conquers her, when in fact he disrobes himself, conquered. Woolf puts Donne beside the "terse and muscular Ben Jonson" (43), whose silent woman, in the play also known as *Epicoene*, is a boy. Inside/outside is figured androgynously, reconfiguring the relations between men and women. Woolf had been doing that from the beginning of *The Common Reader*, providing a "common" canon that joins Chaucer and Margery Paston, that focuses on female characters in *The Canterbury Tales*, in Greek tragedy, and in Jacobean drama. To that end, she closes her Elizabethan explorations with an essay on Margaret Cavendish — a laughingstock in outlandish costumes of her own devising, nonetheless admired by some scientific colleagues, and certainly by her husband who shared with her the belief "'that nobody knew or could know the cause of anything'" (72). Cavendish insisted that everything is some mixture of substance and thought, sense and reason; we have everything in common and yet are each different from each other: "What a rapture is thought" (74). To get mind-boggling thought down on the page defeats the hand that can barely trace out letters that might keep up with the activity of thinking.

To trace the life of the mind in early modern texts Woolf

turns to "this great master of the art of life" (61), Montaigne;
his motto, "*Que sçais-je?*," joins him to the Greeks. Woolf
places him between her Elizabethans and the Duchess of
Newcastle. In more standard accounts of early modern literature, Montaigne, in Florio's translation, would receive
inevitable mention as a Shakespeare source. Shakespeare
plays no great part in her essay on the drama. Montaigne,
a French writer among all these English texts, takes Shakespeare's place; his is an exceptional genius: "This talking
of oneself, following one's own vagaries, giving the whole
map, weight, colour, and circumference of the soul in its
confusion, its variety, its imperfection — that art belonged to
one man only: to Montaigne" (58). His plummeting of the
soul aims at the meaning of life, the life of the mind, to be
sure, but also the art of living. Montaigne's thoughts about
life are recorded in essays to which he continually added af-
terthoughts and marginalia; they are as much reading notes
as they are self-examinations. He finds himself in what he
reads and writes. The movement of his thought, like the
movement of Woolf's, captures "the very pulse and rhythm
of the soul," (67) since "movement and change are the essence of our being" (63). What is his is ours; Montaigne's
sociability — with other people, with books, with us — only
can be recorded as Woolf does, by following his thoughts as
they go astray and yet never wander from this central position: "C'est estre, mais ce ne n'est past vivre, que de se tenir
attaché et obligé par necessité à un seul train" (62; It is existing, but not living, to keep ourselves attached and obliged
by necessity to a single path).

"To communicate is our chief business in life; society
and friendship our chief delights; and reading, not to acquire knowledge, not to earn a living, but to extend our in-
tercourse beyond our own time and province" (64). What
do we know if not that we do not know; Montaigne doubles

back and starts again. We never do catch the soul. She flies
and leads us. "Let death find us at our usual occupations"
(66). That is how one succeeds "in the hazardous enterprise
of living" (67). Not like those creatures in extremis, those
Elizabethan violences, who cry out for death as a relief from
a life that offers only occasions for more violence in objects
at once desired and abhorred. Montaigne takes most anything, takes it or leaves it: "In these extraordinary volumes of
short and broken, long and learned, logical and contradictory statements, we have heard the very pulse and rhythm
of the soul" (67). His soul? Our soul? The life that is. When
we weary of the drama, Woolf opines, "the mind steals off
to muse in solitude" (57). Even then we seek company and
turn "to Donne, to Montaigne, to Sir Thomas Browne, to
the keepers of the keys to solitude" (57). We need them to
unlock the doors to ourselves. "To tell the truth about oneself, to discover oneself near at hand, is not easy" (59). What
is near at hand may not be in our hands entirely. It may be
in the others we are.

The Second Common Reader

Like *The Common Reader*, the *Second Common Reader*
begins with three essays written for it. They comprise the
entirety of Woolf's writing on the early modern period in
the book. Each seeks to understood "the instinct that drives
us" to the Elizabethans, to "become in fancy at least an
Elizabethan," as "The Strange Elizabethans" puts it (9). In
the second, "Donne after Three Centuries," the urgency of
Donne's voice leads us to wonder "what quality the words of
Donne possess that we should hear them distinctly today,"
what "meaning . . . his voice has for us as it strikes upon
the ear after this long flight across the stormy seas that separate us from the age of Elizabeth" (24). "The Countess of

Pembroke's Arcadia" ventures an answer in "our desire" to
escape; it satisfied Sidney and his sister, for whom he wrote
it. "We like to feel that the present is not all" (40).[12]

At first, the motive of escape captivates Woolf in her reading of the *Arcadia*, "where the shepherd is really a prince
and the woman a man; where, in short, anything may be
and happen except what actually is and happens here in England in the year 1580" (41); so, too, the style of writing offers
"to reward the mind that seeks enjoyment for its own sake"
(43). Captivated by the writing, by Sidney's love of words
(and the love of his sister motivating him), Woolf nonetheless finds some traces of a real Sidney in his elaborate
writing, depths of meaning when Pamela understands that a
jewel that Musidorus has given her points in two directions
at once; it suggests the confluence of a real with the fantasy
of the surface. Ultimately here, as in "Notes on an Elizabethan Play," Woolf wearies of the artifice, of plots that go
nowhere. Prose that looks "away from what is actually before
it" (46) is faulted, just as Woolf had faulted *The Defense of
Poesie* in "The Elizabethan Lumber Room."

It is that limit of Elizabethan prose that makes "our"
identification with the "strange Elizabethans" so strange.
Woolf's subject is Gabriel Harvey; she frames "The Strange
Elizabethans" with the story of Harvey's sister, Mercy, and
Philip, Earl of Surrey, who attempted to rape her. Harvey
responded by writing to him "with ambiguous courtesy" to
tell him "that the game was up" (13). Mercy's letters to the
earl also survive; they display her skill and pleasure in writing, "proof that to write was an art, not merely a means of
conveying facts" (14). Impressive in its way, like the *Arcadia*,
it has its limits: "Nothing, one feels, would have been easier for Mercy than to read her lover a fine discourse on the
vanity of grandeur, the loveliness of chastity, the vicissitudes

of fortune. But of emotion as between one particular Mercy and one particular Philip, there is no trace" (14).

"Elizabethan life eludes us" in such writing (15). Harvey's own attempts at using his language as a way to succeed in the Elizabethan world also got him nowhere, except to make him for many a kind of buffoon. Once again Woolf hears something more in his "windy, wordy, voluminous, and obsolete" prose (17), the pride of the poor boy who made himself into a formidable scholar with a passion for poetry. He succeeded in one milieu — around Spenser; for him he created "that atmosphere of hope and ardent curiosity spiced with sound learning that serves to spur the imagination of a young writer and to make each fresh poem as it is written seem the common property of a little band of adventurers set upon the same quest" (19). So, too, finally, Woolf discovers in the hodge-podge of modes of writing in the *Arcadia* — the impersonality of its ancient world, the ordinariness of its clowns, the romance plot in which something more like recognizable emotion appears — "all the seeds of English fiction latent" (49). That is why the book has had something for everyone, from readers in the seventeenth century to our own time. Indeed the "long succession" (40) of readers of the book shows that its value is not bound to any time; it is always capable of being present.

It answers to the potential to become "common property" spelled out in the final essay of the *Second Common Reader*, "How Should One Read a Book?" The title sounds prescriptive, but in the essay Woolf enjoins upon the reader the hard task of maintaining the ability to "enjoy freedom," the freedom to read widely, to learn better what one might expect from every kind of book one might read, to abandon all preconceptions and to work with the words at hand to allow one's mind to remain open; in short, to be readers, not critics. Woolf allows herself a fantasy as she ends; on Judgment Day, St. Peter will say, "These need no reward, We have nothing to give them here. They have loved reading" (270).

"Indeed, it is precisely because we hate and love that our relations with the poets and novelists is so intimate that we find the presence of another person intolerable" (268). The intolerable "other person" here is the critic, who, by telling us what we should think, breaks the intimacy the reader has with what is being read. Harvey succeeded with Sidney and Spenser and in his marginalia, where he wrote "as if he were talking to himself" (20). In his self-communication, the failed public figure became one of those keepers of the keys to a valuable inwardness not one's own but made in dialogue with the books that read him. "Books he loved as a true reader loves them, not as trophies to be hung up for display, but as living beings that 'must be meditated, practised and incorporated into my body and soul'" (23). Books live; they are sites of being, our progenitors.

"'The present tense only to be regarded'" (22) is another bit of Harvey's marginalia that Woolf copies out. The present always present explains how we now might identify with the strange Elizabethans. In her essays on the *Arcadia* and on Harvey, that love is figured as the love between brother and sister, a figuration we recognize from A *Room of One's Own*.[13] In her essay on Donne Woolf finally answers the question of how he manages to be heard now when she finds in his poems to a patroness like the Countess of Bedford something other than the social obsequiousness that marred Harvey's performances even before a queen who found his Italianate good looks appealing.

Before then, Woolf works through the poetic forms and genres Donne engaged and the worlds he created through them. He arrests and shocks us with his aggressivity; nonetheless, "some deeper satisfaction" (25) than mere youthful bravado can be heard in the "momentary intensity" (26) that grabs us, wresting away the assurances of more conventional uses of poetic genres and the social systems they support. In his search for some truth, Donne's insistence on particularity shows the variability of life's phenomena. "It is the union of so many different desires that gives Donne's love poetry not only its vitality but also a quality that is seldom found with such strength in the conventional and orthodox lover — its spirituality" (30). This unity of spirit and flesh shows Donne's "dissatisfaction with the present," his yearning for "a state of unity beyond time, beyond sex, beyond the body" (31). That beyond, however, inheres in bodies, souls — and words. If lovers reach it, it is only momentarily. "Donne snatches the intensity because he is aware of the change that must alter, of the discord that must interrupt" (32).

These intensities make us recognize what else can be made of our lives and through our loves. Taken aback at first by the "servile and obsequious figure" that Donne cut as "the devout servant of the great, the extravagant eulogist of little girls" (32), Woolf reminds herself that these women were learned, that Donne's exercise of extravagant and strange intellectual contortions appealed to their minds. She doesn't have the writing of Lucy, Countess of Bedford, or Magdalen Herbert to prove her point about them as readers who might inspire this writer, so turns to Anne Clifford and her diary for evidence, recalling how the walls of her chambers, like Montaigne's library, were inscribed with writing.[14] These readers lived their reading; Chaucer's "beauteous spirit infuses itself" in her, Clifford writes (34), just as Spenser had declared of himself in *The Faerie Queene* IV.2.34. In his verse letters to women, Donne continues to find another world in this one, "the natural development" from "the personal to the impersonal" (36). The rocket flight of Elizabeth

Drury's soul is Donne's as well. His poems to and about these women prepare Donne to address the God who batters him, to whom he acquiesces, but against whom he also must rebel as the site of contraries inevitably found in mortal existence. Donne rages against life and its limits even as it is within the confines of human existence that he experiences the moments of ecstasy he conveys. There is "no rest, no end, no solution" finally; having Donne we are not done. Woolf glimpses where we are in a final anecdote: "When the fire of London destroyed almost every other monument in St. Paul's, it left Donne's figure untouched, as if the flames themselves found that knot too hard to undo, the riddle too difficult to read, and that figure too entirely itself to turn to common clay" (39). The "figure" to which Woolf refers is literally his statue; figuratively, it is the image of him that lives in his words. The "subtle knot" is also the "subtle not" that makes us human.

Thanks to "new editions and numerous articles," Donne had become a canonical early modern English writer by 1931 (24); he is the only one to whom Woolf devoted an essay in *The Common Reader,* although Margaret Cavendish may serve as a placeholder for the women writers of that age who were not yet canonical, but who might have achieved that status by now (after the hundred years Woolf predicted in *A Room of One's Own* it might take for that to happen). The transformation of "common clay" into something uncommon is something the common reader can perform in reaching from the personal to the impersonal, from this life to the other life we live in reading. "We are in Donne's world now" (25). "Now" is but a moment, as the "as if" ("as if the flames themselves found that knot too hard to undo") with which Woolf figures the power of Donne's figure to ward off a final conflagration suitably chastens us to recognize.

"Anon" / "Moments of Being"

In the final year of her life, Woolf was planning a book tenta-tively titled *Reading at Random* — alternatively, *Turning the Page*.[15] This new book seems to have been conceived at first as a further installment of *The Common Reader*, "a Com-mon History book," Woolf put it in her diary on Septem-ber 12, 1940.[16] Her "Notes for Reading at Random" suggest that she was considering embarking on a more continuous account rather than selecting from published essays and supplementing them. The book would answer the question "What is creation?" (Silver 374) by "explaining lit. from our common standpoint" (375). By "our" here Woolf refers to herself and Vanessa Bell and Duncan Grant. She widens the claim immediately: "We all feel the desire to create." As Brenda Silver points out, this declaration in 1940–41 as bombs fell (one destroying the Woolfs's London residence), expressed "the urgency of Woolf's need to equate the instinct to create with the instinct of self-preservation and commu-nal survival" (381). "Take a living book," Woolf proposes to herself, and through that germ find a way to imagine life that goes on, "the continuity of tradition" (373), "the universality of the creative instinct" (376).

On November 23, having finished drafting *Between the Acts*, Woolf turned "to write the first chapter of the next book (nameless). Anon, it will be called" (Diary 5:340). Woolf's name for the nameless book — "Anon" — titles the chapter Woolf drafted. "Anon" remained unpublished until Silver edited a text from the drafts, appending to it the few pages completed of the next essay, "The Reader." The two together define the parameters of writing without a name. Woolf lo-cates "the germ of creation" in "a very old anon. poem" (376) and begins "Anon" with such a text; "Anon" recognizes its voice in a bird singing and overcomes species and language difference in the poem. "Anon" is not singular, but "sometimes man; sometimes woman, the common voice singing out of doors" (382). By the end of "Anon," "the audience is replaced by the reader." The reader is an indoor creature, taking in things through the eye, not the ear. "Anon is dead" (398). Yet, on the same page, a couple of paragraphs before that decisive ending, Woolf affirms that the "nameless vitality" that animated Anon is "not yet dead in ourselves." "We can still become anonymous."

"It was the printing press that finally was to kill Anon. But it was the press also that preserved him" (384) in words that continue to resonate on the page. That life can be any of ours — as readers — and as the collective of common readers who share that common possibility. "The anonymous world to which we can still return" precedes "us" before we become conscious of ourselves as individual selves; it will return us to "the world beneath our consciousness" (385) that, it appears, lives in words that precede and survive our existence. This is "the kingdom of our own language," as Gabriel Harvey wrote in a letter to Spenser that Woolf cites in "Anon" (390).

Words "seem able to live for ever," Woolf proposed in "Craftsmanship," a talk she gave on April 20, 1937 (printed posthumously in 1942 by Leonard Woolf).[17] They don't have a singular meaning but intimate "a thousand possibilities" (171); hence "they combine unconsciously together" (173); "they do not live in dictionaries; they live in the mind" (176). The writer should let words be and not attempt to pin them down to one meaning. What we know about words, Woolf opines, "is that they seem to like people to think and to feel before they use them, but to think and feel not about them, but about something different" (170). That "something different," Gilles Deleuze claims, is life itself.[18] Words must be allowed their life; to fly away from us in order to remain with us: "When words are pinned down they fold their wings and die" (177).

In "Anon," Woolf locates Spenser on the threshold that separates him from past anonymity and makes him beholden to readers. In "The Reader," Woolf notes that reading enhances our ability to see more than is apparent on the page. With Spenser, "we are in a world where nothing is concluded" (429); Spenser the writer also is a reader of Chaucer: "He must have heard something rising, bursting up, from beneath," "half in shadow, half in light" (391). Spenser hears and recreates "the voice at the back door" (392), Anon's voice, unsocialized, untamed, unplaced. Woolf hears it in *The Faerie Queene*. "There is no tension; no direction; but always movement, as the metre flings its curve of sound, to break, like a wave in the same place, and like a wave to withdraw, to fill again; yet always we see through the waters, something irradiated" (391), a description of the endless energy of Spenser's epic spelled out in Woolf's brief essay, "The Faery Queen," written after spending the first six months of 1935 reading the epic. (Woolf's essay was published posthumously by Leonard Woolf in *The Moment* [1947]).[19] Spenser appears frequently in "Notes for Reading at Random": "something very deep — primitive. Not yet extinct. The eye. Spenser" (377). "The eye of the mind opens," she writes in "The Faery Queen" (487); the poem captivates us at every level of mind and body: "The tree must be part of the knight; the knight of the lady. All these states of mind must support one another." "The mind is being perpetually enlarged by the power of suggestion. Much more is imagined than is stated" (488). "We feel that the whole being is drawn upon": that being is the poet's, "alive in all its parts" (489), and ours as well. It "still corresponds to something which we who are momentarily in the flesh feel at the moment" (488). Spenser wrote at a specific historical juncture, but the moment of his poem is not just the product of that time; enunciated on a "depersonalised scale," it is more realistic than the realism we may think we want from literature (489). An allegorical personification of Spenser's "draws natural breath, living breath." Hence, "it is easier to read Spenser than to read William Morris" (490); the Elizabethans are closer to us than are the Victorians. "We are uncabined" (488), taken out of ourselves in Spenser; "On no other terms . . . could we be kept in being . . . we live in a great bubble blown from the poet's brain. . . . So we feel not shut in, but freed; and take our way in a world which gives expression to sensation more vigorously, more exactly than we can manage for ourselves in the flesh" (491). In these words, Woolf sums up what it means for us to live as readers, the moment of being in that other life of ours.

Woolf uses the phrase "moments of being" in her autobiographical "A Sketch of the Past" (composed between April 1939 and November 1940) to describe feelings of "great intensity" from the past that "can still be more real than the present moment."[20] "Is it not possible — I often wonder — that things we have felt with great intensity have an existence independent of our minds; are in fact still in existence?" (67). Those feelings, while had by someone, do not feel as if they arise from self-awareness; they are more like ecstasy and rapture, the feeling of being outside oneself and yet inside something. "We are sealed vessels afloat on what it is convenient to call reality; and at some moments, the sealing matter cracks; in floods reality" (122). The crack is a shock; one reality replaces another. We become aware that we have "not lived consciously" (70); moments of being show us that most of our lived lives are moments of what Woolf calls nonbeing. Being and non-being mark the distinction Montaigne drew between existing and living.

Moments of being are the "origin of . . . [Woolf's] writing impulse" (122); she makes these moments "real by . . . words" (72). This is why, as Woolf supposed in "Craftsmanship," words "like us . . . to become unconscious" (171); they can speak for us about what we cannot know consciously. Writing can "make it whole" by "discovering what belongs to what" (72), intimating what is behind, beneath what we think of as real. "All human beings" are "connected with this." The "whole world is a work of art; . . . we are parts of the work of art" (72). Woolf exemplifies that "work of art" in the life of a plant as it grows "up out of the earth, up until the stalk grows, the leaf grows, the bud swells." It is always changing and yet always driven by "the force of life" (79) that persists. "*Hamlet* or a Beethoven quartet is the truth about this vast mass that we call the world. But there is no Shakespeare, there is no Beethoven and emphatically there is no God; we are the words; we are the music; we are the thing itself" (73).

These astonishing declarations about what we are Woolf knew in the rapture of creation, the experience she recounts about *To the Lighthouse*. Walking in Tavistock Square, the novel came to her "in a great, apparently involuntary, rush. One thing burst into another. Blowing bubbles out of a pipe gives the feeling of the rapid crowd of ideas and scenes which blew out of my mind, so that my lips seemed syllabling of their own accord as I walked. What blew these bubbles? Why then? I have no notion" (81). This also is the rapture she felt in reading: "I read Shakespeare *directly* I have finished writing, when my mind is agape & red & hot. Then it is astonishing. I never yet knew how amazing his stretch & speed and word coining power is, until I felt it utterly outpace & outrace my own. . . . Why then should anyone else attempt to write. This is not 'writing' at all. Indeed, I could say that Sh[akespea]re surpasses literature altogether, if I knew what I meant."[21] Shakespeare finds words that discover what we do not know but are. He is not himself. We are what we are not: the thing itself, anonymous.

3

Ambiguous Empson

Seven Types of Ambiguity and Some Versions of Pastoral

"A living matter . . ."

In his 1947 preface to the second edition of *Seven Types of Ambiguity*, William Empson addresses questions about his book that critics had raised in the years since it first appeared in 1930. Responding to a 1931 review of the book by James Smith, Empson feels that it offers him a way to address "the fundamental arguments against . . . [his] approach."[1] He homes in on the central paragraphs of Smith's review, which opened with a remarkably cogent paragraph summary of Empson's seven types. Measured praise and exceptions to some of Empson's examples follow; Smith ends by acknowledging Empson's "unusually brilliant" insights (45). In his 1947 preface, Empson ponders a review by an adversary capable of appreciating his work. And vice versa: in "Double Plots," the longest essay in *Some Versions of Pastoral* (1935;

the title of that essay could apply to Empson's oeuvre in general), Empson refers admiringly to a 1933 essay by Smith on metaphysical poetry. In 1947, Empson was answering a critic with whom he shared assumptions.[2] Both of them, it appears, were of two minds.

Smith's worries about *Seven Types of Ambiguity* include one about "scale." He faults Empson for using identical methods for interpreting drama as poetry; Empson concedes (and justifies) his procedures as "one of those necessary simplifications, without which indeed life could not go forward, but which are always breaking down" (xiii), a response in terms of "life" that leaves unsaid much in question. His answer relates to another of Smith's worries (one that Empson answers more fully) — that his definition of "ambiguity," which, as Smith acknowledges, is "necessarily vague" (43) to permit a wide-ranging inquiry, is too vague; it ignores, for instance, the obvious distinction between concision and ambiguity. Smith's main concern is that Empson fails at the basic task of literary criticism, the delivery of "a judgement of value" (xii; this criterion marks the influence of F. R. Leavis). Empson quotes most of the paragraph in which Smith makes this point as well as the next one, which recapitulates the problem of "his vagueness as to the nature and scope of ambiguity" (xii). These lead Smith to a conclusion that raises his fundamental question: "Is the ambiguity referred to that of life — is it a bundle of diverse forces, bound together only by their co-existence? Or is it that of a literary device . . . ? If the first, Mr. Empson's thesis is wholly mistaken; for a poem is not a mere fragment of life, it is a fragment that has been detached, considered, and judged by a mind. A poem is a noumenon rather than a phenomenon. If the second, then at least we can say that Mr. Empson's thesis is exaggerated" (xii).

Empson's response to the Kantian dichotomy that he takes

Smith to pose, "noumenon or a phenomenon" (xv), seems
almost hinted in Smith's either/or; it suggests the possibility
of answering "both/and." It's easy to imagine that as Empson's answer, since it was the critical position he claimed in
Seven Types of Ambiguity to have found offered "in the Arden
text" of Shakespeare (81), multiple possibilities of meaning,
rather than in the either/or the Arden editors might have expected readers to choose. Empson reimagines Shakespeare's
canonical power as found not in what he really meant but
in what the text can say. Helen Thaventhiran has identified
this as crucial to Empson's critical practice.[3] "I have myself
usually said 'either . . . or'," in response to these prompts,
Empson notes, "when meaning 'both . . . and'" (81). Empson takes both positions, both "either . . . or" and "both . . .
and." Ambiguity leaves in question — as ambiguous — the
distinctions that Smith would have him make. Empson's
answers in his 1947 preface echo his response to Smith in
"Double Plots." He refers to him there as "a reviewer of my
book on ambiguity" who "rightly said that I was confusing
poetical with dramatic uses of it, which he said showed that
I was treating poems as phenomena not as things judged
by a mind" (67). The trouble with that distinction, Empson
goes on to say, is that the mind is not singular; it includes
the ability to judge but also to be inspired "to mean more"
than one knows consciously. The mind's ability to withdraw
from what it sees to generalize fundamental truths that include all possible instantiations faces "an insoluble puzzle
because the two are mutually dependent, like the One and
the Many" (68). "The mind is complex and ill-connected
like an audience" (68), like Shakespeare's audience. A few
pages later, in "Double Plots," Empson names "Mr. James
Smith," who proposed "that the metaphysical conceit was
always built out of the immediate realisation of a philosophical problem such as that of the One and the Many" (80), the

terms Empson had invoked in his earlier response to Smith's
critique. In "On Metaphysical Poetry," Smith wrote about
the "insoluble problem" of mutual dependency as Empson
does: "The contradictions in metaphysics . . . spring from essence. The very nature of things brings them forth. It seems
impossible that the nature of things should possess either the
one or the other of a pair of qualities; it seems impossible
that it should possess both together; it seems impossible that
it should not possess both" (227).

What is both possible and impossible in "the very nature
of things" seems likewise to be the case with poetry, even if
a poem is not a phenomenon but an object of thought. Toward the end of *Seven Types of Ambiguity* Empson ponders
"the mode of action of poetry" (243); poetry is not something there on the page, not a thing, nor is it something
set randomly in the company of other things that exist; it
is in motion — alive, in relation, never exactly self-identical
to itself, always therefore more than singular in its singularity. (Likewise, every performance of Shakespeare is Shakespeare; every edition is, too, although all differ from each
other.) "It might seem more reasonable, when dealing with
obscure alternatives of syntax," Empson continues, "to abandon the claim that you are explaining a thing communi-
cated," and instead to try to locate the poem as an object
in the author's mind or in the reader's. This does not solve
the problem; it only locates more axes of ambiguity. The
ontological status of the poetic object is in question precisely
because, Empson goes on to say, "it is a living matter" (245).
It can't be regarded as a detached noumenon, an object of
thought; nor can it be put into other words supposedly less
opaque than those found in the poem. It lives this coexis-
tence with and as what at the same time it is, a detached and
shaped fragment of a presumed whole; its life is refiguration.

To illustrate this claim, toward the end of his 1947 preface Empson mentions a recent exhibit of some studies by Constable, works that he never personally exhibited. Critics were hailing these as far more significant than the works that the artist regarded as finished; those on display were, for him, sketches tied too closely to the objects that inspired him. "Would Mr. James Smith say that the 'study,' which is now more admired than the finished work, was a noumenon or a phenomenon?" (xv), Empson asks. There is no definitive answer to this question. Moreover, Empson further notes, the present overturning of Constable's (and his contemporaries') sense about what a Constable is may be true in 1947, but will not necessarily be so later. Like works of art, literature is "a living matter" "because, insofar as people are always reading an author, he is always being read differently" (245). Literature that lasts — or that comes back — or that at first seems strange and unreadable, but then is read and reread — lives many lives. And why not if the author or the reader is likely to be of at least two minds. The mind is capable of withdrawing to judge and shape; the mind can be caught by what it does not know is there. Empson insists that finding a poem beautiful initiates a critical process that does not end at judgment, but seeks to understand what makes the work beautiful. Ambiguity inheres in all "good poetry" (xv) to which one is attracted enough to seek to find "the secret places of the Muse" (196); its not so secret truth is that "human life is so much a matter of juggling with contradictory impulses" (197) that "the human situation is oddly riddled with . . . antinomies" (249). Poems are desituated situations where "the most complicated and deeply rooted notion of the mind" (233) can be found, as Empson avers of George Herbert's "The Sacrifice" at the end of *Seven Types of Ambiguity*. "Unless you are enjoying the poetry you cannot create it, as poetry, in your mind" (248). Rational judgment of value supposes an impossible division between subject and object along with the singularity of the judging mind. It supposes that the analysis of a poem turns it into prose. Rather, Empson affirms (it is his last word in *Seven Types of Ambiguity*), critical thought "makes poetry more beautiful" (256).

Any poem can be received by any mind. What is received in each instance is not the same thing. Prompted by Herbert's "Hope," Empson avers in *Seven Types of Ambiguity* to explain that "generalisations act like this" — they tumble together ambiguities. Empson attempts to categorize separable types, but categories cannot hold, if only for the obvious reason that close reading does not happen all at once; one returns again and again to a text that one finds compelling and that is not yet exhausted by a single reading. Of "Hope," Empson concludes, "one may say, then, that in ordinary careful reading this poem is of the third type, but when you know it sufficiently well, and have accepted it, it becomes an ambiguity of the first (or since it is verbally ingenious) of the second type" (121).[4] Generalization is itself ambiguous. Temporal spacing into "ors" quickly becomes "ands"; noumenon and phenomenon won't stay put because whatever the supposed subject of a good poem may be "throws light on matters of another sort, because it illustrates life, or what not" (121). When a reader, Empson concludes in 1947, "is seriously moved" by a poem, "what are moving in him are the traces of a great part of his past experience and of the structure of his past judgments" (xv). Being of two minds at once, moved by both experience and judgment, life and thought, past and present, reading leads to a condition that only can be described ambiguously — "so straddling a commotion and so broad a calm," (xv) Empson ventures in his 1947 preface "a releasing and knotted duality" (132) in *Seven Types of Ambiguity*.

"An example from one of Mr. Waley's Chinese translations"

Seven Types of Ambiguity is a book almost entirely about canonical works of English literature (Shakespeare at its center); perhaps to show the limits of that framework, early in the book, Empson offers two lines identified only as Arthur Waley's translation from the Chinese to encapsulate the essential work of poetic ambiguity:[5]

Swiftly the years, beyond recall.
Solemn the stillness of this spring morning.

(23)

These lines show that "the human mind has two main scales on which to measure time": "human life as its unit, the years one has to live," about which there is "nothing to be done" but accept them as given (24); the other, life as "the conscious moment," to which is attached "absolute or extra-temporal value," as if death might be forestalled, stilled, controlled, absorbed. Between these two — a full life, a full second — the scale is extreme; both are in these lines. The words that mark them, "swiftly" and "stillness," provide "a single apprehension" in which the long and short views cross: the brief morning takes on the serenity of the accepted full life; life at its end seems scarcely to have begun. The words that qualify "years" and "this spring morning" behave the way adjectives do, comparatively, as Empson explains in the final chapter of *Seven Types of Ambiguity*: "An adjective . . . can always imply its opposite elsewhere" (203). This observation fits Empson's initial definition of ambiguity: "any verbal nuance, however slight, which gives room for alternative reactions to the same piece of language" (1). Nothing stands alone; not a single word. In Waley's lines, two opposite words "being contradictory as they stand . . .

demand to be conceived in different ways; we are enabled, therefore, to meet the open skies with an answering stability of self-knowledge; to meet the brevity of human life with an ironical sense that it is morning and springtime, that there is a whole summer before winter, a whole day before night." This is "the essential fact about the poetical use of language": "Two statements are made as if they were connected, and the reader is forced to consider their relationship for himself" (25). Empson explains this finally through claims about the history of thought and language: "Opposite is a comparatively late human invention" (192). Following Freud on the antithetical sense of primal words (the language of the unconscious), Empson proposes that originally languages used the same word for what we take to be opposites. His examples include Latin *altus* for "high" and "low"; the Egyptian hieroglyph that means "baby" and "old man"; "let," which in Elizabethan English means both "allow" and "stop." "In short, as you know that two things are opposites, you know a relation which connects them" (196). That fundamental ambiguous situation joins phenomenon and noumenon. It drives home "the fundamental commonplace of poetry, a statement of the limitations of the human situation" (73).

"The experience of accepting the poetry"

In both *Seven Types of Ambiguity* and *Some Versions of Pastoral*, early modern English literature is at the center of Empson's attention. That period, he says toward the end of *Seven Types of Ambiguity*, "seems to have been curiously free from such critical principles as interpose a judgment before the experience of accepting the poetry is completed" (241). Empson claims that seventeenth-century poets were "responsible for most of the ambiguities" he finds in the poetry. The language made this possible: early modern English allowed undifferentiated spellings of words that became differentiated; later notions of correctness did not prevail; grammar that allowed a line of poetry to refer back and ahead at once was valued; punctuation was rhetorical, not syntactical. In his 1947 preface to *Seven Types of Ambiguity*, Empson described his task, prompted by T. S. Eliot, he says, to be a "consideration of the claims of nineteenth-century poets so as to get them into perspective with the newly discovered merits of Donne, Marvell, and Dryden" (viii). Empson's way of doing that was not Eliot's blanket of exclusions, but rather inclusion: he demonstrates the logical consistency of Shelley's seemingly vague imagery, underscores the appeal of Wordsworth's pantheism, unearths ambiguity in the self-conscious wit of Pope, admires the "subdued conceits and ambiguities" of Swinburne (165). Marvell may have been a new discovery in the 1920s; he had not been forgotten before, but "read . . . in different ways" (173). So, too, with Crashaw: Empson's focus is on the imbrication of sexuality and spirituality in his poems; readers who find this makes his poetry beautiful "are reading it in a very different way from others who would agree with them" about its beauty without countenancing what Empson saw (220).

As soon as Empson launches his way into proliferating types of ambiguity "as belonging to the later stages of Renaissance refinement" (57), he stops and starts again with Chaucer's *Troilus and Criseyde* for a dozen pages. While he always returns to early modernity, it remains the proliferating omphalos of his inquiry. The climatic conclusion to *Seven Types of Ambiguity*, Empson's reading of Herbert's "The Sacrifice," proceeds from Keats's "Ode to Melancholy" through Crashaw and the "buckle" of tying and releasing in Hopkins's Windhover. Waley's translation, fastening on the central ambiguity of all poetry, is followed immediately by lines by Nashe and Jonson; Milton, Pope, and Shakespeare are among those who come before.

The lives that poems can have and live to convey is the one we imagine. We think existence unending even as we know that we must die, just as we know that life on this planet will cease to exist; life will nonetheless persist, perhaps in some other universe, but not necessarily in a form any of us would recognize.[6]

"A summer's day . . ." (Milton)

Pages before the Waley example of two seemingly disconnected images that exercise the reader to find what connects them, Empson cites, as an example of the calming effect that reconciliation can have, these lines about Mulciber from *Paradise Lost* (1.741 ff.):

> thrown by angry Jove
> Sheer o'er the crystal battlements; from morn
> To noon he fell, from noon to dewy eve,
> A summer's day; and with the setting sun
> Dropped from the zenith — (p.12)

"It is delightfully soothing to feel that the devil is all the time falling faster and faster," Empson notes; it also is the case that his fall is smoothed and slows down as it traces an arc from morn to noon, from noon to evening, before it drops, pulled by a gravitational force that seemed relaxed for a while. The possibility of rising again, as the sun will to complete its circular arc, also can be imagined.

Empson includes Milton in *Seven Types of Ambiguity*, accommodating him to the new wonders of Donne. He also compares him several times to Shakespeare; puns in *Paradise Lost, Paradise Regained,* and *Samson Agonistes* located at "the intersections between separated parts of the mind" raise "questions of consciousness" (102). In the lines about Mulciber, Empson overlooks what might disquiet a mind: the pun on "eve" that could connect her with the plot engineered by "angry Jove." Those are complications he engages in "Milton and Bentley" in *Some Versions of Pastoral*. Empson reiterated and expanded his argument there in his final book, almost thirty years later, *Milton's God*.

Empson opens "Milton and Bentley" by demurring from Woolf's dismissal of the eighteenth-century critic in *The Common Reader*. He sees rather that Bentley's insistence that *Paradise Lost* is filled with lines that Milton couldn't possibly have written, and must have had foisted upon him, allows him to unearth ambiguities and irresolutions that rankle his desire to normalize Milton's poem. Bentley catches Milton out when of two minds about justifying the ways of God. Milton's monism, his refusal of an absolute distinction between the physical and the spiritual, concrete and abstract, baffle Bentley; life and death are thereby put in question, made to hang on an apple, as Satan snarls derisively, "a fearful source of revelation," Empson notes (187). Milton gives "every action a nightmare importance. . . . It is a terrific fancy, the Western temper at its height; the insane disproportion of the act to its effects" (181). Somewhere in Milton's mind is the thought "that the human creature is essentially out of place in the world and needed no fall in time to make him so" (186).

"If Milton's sympathies were divided, he understood the conflict he was dramatising, and if the result is hard to explain, it is easy to feel," Empson urges (153); Bentley seizes what is hard, maybe impossible, fully to understand. He is stymied by the angel eating with Adam and Eve; Empson agrees it shows the "absurd" lengths Milton goes to tell his pastoral story. The "insane disproportion" that Milton tries to justify begins in the opening lines of *Paradise Lost* that couple "fruit" with death and with the restoration to life through the replacement of Adam with the "greater man." Empson looks askance at the "appalling God" (168) who jokingly encourages Satan to doubt his omnipotence and pretends to be unsure he will find a volunteer to sacrifice himself for the couple he made free to fall. None of his supposed created beings seems to know the game he is playing with them; Satan might well be sincerely seeking to rescue Adam and Eve from their inevitable suffering. It's not his apparent lot as he flies free.

Empson links the portrayal of Eve to the wrenching sacrifice of "paganism" required by Christianity. The pastoral world exists for her "vilification" (172), "Eve-baiting" (174) that suggests that she is fallen before the fall, Satan's seducer: "Eve was Delilah, the more specious for her innocence" (177). The same thing happens to the pastoral world in the lines about Mulciber. They end with Mulciber as a "falling star" lands "On Lemnos the Aegean isle"; the pastoral tale is immediately dismissed as a false fable: "Thus they relate,/Erring; for he with this rebellious rout/Fell long before" (1.745–48). In *Seven Types of Ambiguity*, Empson stops his consolatory story before these lines. In *Some Versions of Pastoral*, he takes up the star story, tracing across Milton's oeuvre the "curious parallel between Satan and Christ" (165) that Bentley called out when the devil regrets his "incarnate" state as a serpent (9.166). By *Paradise Regained*, Jesus is the Morning Star Lucifer, cementing "Milton's secret parallel between the two" (183). This parallel also, Empson avers, is Milton's story: "Satan is Milton as rebel and also the paganism Milton had renounced" (169). "Surely Bentley was right to be surprised at finding Faunus haunting the bower" (190); Milton voices what he had to renounce in order to believe, but not without doubting Christian mythology; "the reverberations of this doubt are the real subject of the description of the Garden" (177). "Milton identified Satan with part of his own mind" (172); as both "the punisher of sin and the supreme sinner" (169), God frees Satan to do his bidding.

"Thus they relate, Erring"; to err means to go astray but also to wander on a path that may not be the wrong one, the way knights errant roam. Milton's "complex feelings about Paradise" (172) plot such a course; Bentley, Empson argues, sought to emend and to remove the ambiguity of Milton's double situation. Edenic melancholy is linked to the insoluble "puzzles about the knowledge, freedom, happiness, and strength of the state of innocence, but applied to the original innocence of Nature" (187). The apple tests what Abdiel claims, that "God and Nature bid the same" (6.176). That sentence poses questions about the relationship between humans and God, the physical and the spiritual — questions about the difference and connection of feeling/intuiting and what we know to doubt, the life we have to lose, and the one we think originally ours.

Empson's brief citation from *Paradise Lost* in the first chapter of *Seven Types of Ambiguity* involves the temporal juxtaposition about one's life that Empson illuminates in Waley's translation. "One is made to sit with him pleasantly in the shade, all day long, needing no further satisfaction": this is the time we had in the garden we first were given when we were created to be immortal. "It is delightfully soothing to feel that the devil is falling faster and faster," Empson continues, as if he has been fully routed and rendered impotent (12). Yet, when readers ponder our safety in this shaded point of view, we can't help but recall that what our minds go on thinking is belied by the story Milton tells; in it we sought more satisfaction from the garden in the fruit that "angry Jove" forbade us; eating it made us mortal, as he knew would happen. That counterstory is in the lines, too; the fall of the devil comes as the sun sets. We enter into the dark night of mortal existence and a son sacrificed to make the story fortunate, as if we were still sitting in the garden, now, but in our minds, a paradise within, happier far in our mortal bodies, knowing that there is more to life than death. We are prepared to think through our error.

"Pouring immortality in a cramped, trying script on the page" (Shakespeare)

In his review of *Seven Types of Ambiguity*, Smith commended Empson for tracing the pun "from Milton, Dryden and the Augustans" (42); he reserves his most generous praise for Empson's "work on Shakespeare" (44). In this, he is not alone. Michael Wood opens his recent *On Empson* by pondering "a moment" when Empson "decides to linger in Macbeth's mind."[7] Wood ties almost all of his appreciations of Empson's critical acuity to readings of early modern texts, Shakespeare most frequently. He initially explains this by characterizing Empson as "a good disciple of John Donne as Eliot saw him" (17), but it's worth noting that in his lifelong engagement with Shakespeare, as in his with Milton, Empson was not modeling himself on Eliot. Empson subjects Shakespeare to his own mode of analysis of ambiguity. Wood acutely describes this when he notes that Empson's occupation of Macbeth's mind involves "finding metaphors for the behavior of a piece of language" (3). Empson is after "the life of these words" (4); it only can be captured through other words, ideally, as Empson writes, in a response that is itself a kind of poem that registers one's full engagement in what one reads — mind and body, thought and feeling — noumenon and phenomenon in their inextricable ambiguous relationship.

Wood cites a few lines from Macbeth's soliloquy that opens, "If it were done when 'tis done, then 'twere well/It were done quickly" (1.7.1–2). Empson pauses to note the possibility that the first line is endstopped and thus an example of "double syntax" (49) characteristic of the second type of ambiguity before he continues to the lines that most engage him: "if th' assassination/Could trammel up the consequence, and catch/With his surcease, success." In them Empson hears "words hissed in the passage where servants were passing, which must be swaddled in darkness" (the sounds suggest the allusion to the naked babe transformed, cloaked in this whispered hissing, "not made too naked even to his mind" [50]). The words begin to live their own life; the naked babe is soon found in "*catch*, the single little flat word among these monsters" (50). "Catch" tries to stop the ramifying consequences (surcease lives beyond stopping and success marks an end that never ends; the monster is a life that continues); the catch in "catch" is that "it is a mark of human inadequacy . . . , a child snatching at the moon as she rides thunder-clouds." Empson does not stop here because "the meanings cannot all be remembered at once" (50). His metaphors, made in part from Shakespeare's, literally re-member them as he attempts to catch as many meanings as possible in this ambiguous situation without an end.

This moment in Macbeth's mind with which Wood begins was not the first time Empson put himself there; in the first chapter of *Seven Types of Ambiguity*, contemplating the lines Macbeth speaks to Lady Macbeth at the end of 3.2, Empson focuses on Macbeth's invocation of night; he sees him looking out a window while "light thickens; and the crow/Makes wing to th' rooky wood" (50–51); light thickens like the witches' brew or coagulating blood. Empson reads these lines as one in which Macbeth sees himself as "the peaceful solitary *crow*" and, at the same time, "unnaturally like . . . a murderer who is coming against them" (19). Is he akin to the "good things of the day" or "night's black agents," a crow or a raven, or a pun that combines them?

Empson recurs to this puzzle at the end of chapter one, finding it spaced between the lines of the messenger bringing the news that the first promise of the witches has been fulfilled without Macbeth doing anything to assume the title of Thane of Cawdor and Macbeth's horror at what he has done to make the second promise true. The messenger had told Macbeth that Duncan rewards him with Cawdor's title for his fearlessness against the Norwegian foes, "Nothing afeard of what thyself did make,/Strange images of death" (1.3. 96–97). By 2.2.50, fearlessness becomes fear. He has killed the king and describes himself as "afraid to think what I have done." Empson suggests that we don't have "to remember one when hearing the other" lines (45). Maybe. We might recall that Milton used Duncan's lines, proclaiming his son his heir, as the model for God's announcement, inciting Satan as Macbeth had been.

By the second chapter of *Seven Types of Ambiguity*, after Empson translates "or" into "and" as the way we can attempt to "bear in mind all the meanings" and find "our way back" to Shakespeare's "original meaning" (82), the possibility of not connecting opposing lines no longer seems on offer. What Shakespeare does "casts a new light on the very nature of language" (80), Empson claims. Wood shares the excitement that the rooky wood holds forth; Empson means by "original meaning" the "simultaneous presence of many meanings" (47). He takes this insight, too, from Empson's analysis of statues of the Buddha's face that he began writing at about the same time he was writing *Some Versions of Pastoral*; in them, the two halves do not match, although the asymmetry is not apparent. They are "figures who have left the world and still belong to it," Wood writes (53). One could say something similar to describe what Macbeth sees seeing himself in the birds out the window as day turns into night; or to describe Empson, putting himself in Macbeth's mind and finding there a language of originary twoness; Shakespeare's "original meaning" pours "immortality in a cramped, trying hand," Empson writes (84). His hand, cramped by multiples, left baffling marks that editors try to unravel, struggling to comprehend what came to Shakespeare all at once. This is the "immortality" of language that the human mind can think.

Empson tries his hand at that topic through *Macbeth* again in chapter seven, glancing at Macbeth as he tries to accept what will happen after the witches' first prophecy comes true: "Come what come may/Time and the hour runs through the roughest day" (1.3.147–48). He contemplates what may happen, accepting it if he wants it, not worrying if he doesn't. "These opposites may be paired with predestination and freewill," Empson comments, linking *Macbeth* to the central thematic of *Paradise Lost*. He paraphrases Macbeth's thought this way: "Whatever I do, even if and when I kill him, the sensible world will go on" (201). Life never ceases. The doublet "time and the hour" suggests this too to Empson: "two opposed impulses, towards control . . . towards yielding" (201) cross, as they did in Waley's lines — the life we know that always is and the one we know we will not always have.

Dr. Johnson called the pun Shakespeare's "fatal Cleopatra"; he succumbed to it much as Adam did to Eve. "It might, I think, be possible to relate a poet's attitude to life with his attitude to words," Empson notes about the pun (it provoked Johnson's worry about Shakespeare's masculinity) as he concludes his discussion of how "or" really is "and," how therefore opposition is not any different from apposition, fate from free will, choosing from not choosing.

Empson does not summon up the Buddha heads to illustrate his point (as he might well have done), but "the precisely similar extravagant gestures with which the Ganymedes and the Titans of Michael Angelo express respectively
their yielding and their power" (87).

This embodied gesture of yielding power, binding similarity and difference, could be put beside Virginia Woolf's
androgyny; Empson locates it in the words Shakespeare uses
and the ambiguity of his grammar, "in which phrases will go
either with the sentence before or after"; they make for the
"interpenetrating and, as it were, fluid unity" (50) of the sonnets (Smith quotes this description of Empson's admiringly
in his review). "Donne . . . uses these methods with a vehemence," Empson continues, quickly glancing at lines from
an epithalamium (51) before returning to pages of examples
from Shakespeare's sonnets. He opens his analysis of type 4
ambiguity with a characteristic close reading of forward/
backward syntax in sonnet 83 as it arrives at the declaration,
"For I impair not beauty, being mute/When others would
give life, and bring a tomb" (11–12). Empson finds in this life/
death ambiguity a sign of the "generosity" that Shakespeare
shows to the fair young man. "Shakespeare includes the
whole ambiguity in his enthusiasm; the worth and the sin,
the beauty and painting, all are delightful to him, and too
subtle to be grasped" (139). Instead of eulogizing the young
man as a means to praise him, the sonneteer accepts him as
he is; this "mysterious . . . totality" is, at once, among "the
effects of language" and "the composition of feeling, which
never falls apart among these ambiguities (it is, on any interpretation, pained, bitter, tender and admiring; Shakespeare
is being abandoned by W. H., and stiffly apologizing for not
having been servile to him)" (138–39). Empson follows Oscar Wilde in dubbing the young man "W. H."

"Simply the thing I am / Shall make me live"

In his 1956 essay "The Dead-End of Formalist Criticism," Paul de Man singled out Empson from other "New Critics," British and American as well as French, for his acute awareness of the constitutive role of language in poetry.[8] De Man takes from Shakespeare his "very first example" from those that Empson offers, "mainly," de Man notes, "though not exclusively, from Shakespeare and the metaphysical poets of the seventeenth century" (235). It is the first citation in *Seven Types of Ambiguity*, a line from sonnet 73: "Bare ruined choirs, where late the sweet birds sang" (2). De Man admires what Empson suggests, its "vibration spreading in infinitude from its center, metaphor . . . endowed with the capacity to situate the experience at the heart of a universe that it generates . . . a limitless anteriority that permits the limiting of a specific entity" (235). The generative life of the poem, its "vibration," arises from a body likened in the opening lines of the sonnet to an autumnal tree losing its leaves. Empson describes the line's metaphoricity as a "synthesis" that delivers "a sudden perception of an objective relation," more readily available to analysis than the situation itself might be, through the "fundamental situation" of "a grammatical structure . . . effective in several ways at once" (2).

"Bare ruined choirs, where late the sweet birds sang": the line leaps suddenly from the tree to which the aging sonneteer had likened himself to the song of the birds. What de Man calls the vibrancy of the line Empson describes as its effect, what it does. "Choirs" glances back at the tree insofar as church choirs are made of wood and located in buildings perhaps like those ruined in the dissolution of the monasteries; not made of wood, they were "crystallized out of the likeness of a forest" in their carvings and stained-glass

images (3). Empson doesn't mention the aptness of singing
for the former activity of the sonneteer ("*cano*," famously,
is Virgil's term for writing), instead linking the bird song
to choir boys and thereby to W. H., who shares their "cold
and Narcissistic charm" (3). Empson's synthesis draws the
male couple together, much as the sonneteer hopes that
W. H. may see in his love and through his metaphors the
mortality they share. The poem makes the connection in
a punning tautology; a few "leaves" may yet remain on the
tree; the young man will "leave" him when he dies, if not
more immediately.

All these implications and more can be unpacked in the
beauty of the metaphor, "and there is a sort of ambiguity
in not knowing which of them to hold in mind," Empson
continues; these "machinations . . . are among the very roots
of poetry." A singular meaning is "hard to isolate" (3). De
Man concurs: the "imaging activity . . . does not 'mean' in
any definite manner" (235) when an "infinite plurality of sig-
nifications" are "melded into a single linguistic unit" (236).
Nonetheless, Empson takes a stab at one kind of meaning
sonnet 73 delivers: "There is a sort of meaning, the sort that
people are thinking when they say 'this poet will mean more
to you when you have had more experience of life'" (3). That
experience may coincide with the Hegelian "unhappy consciousness" that de Man associates with poetic utterance, its
realization that "the spirit cannot coincide with the object,"
since the latter only can be known "in its dissolution into
non-being" (237). Empson approaches sonnet 73 much as he
does when he sums up his generous/generative analysis of
sonnet 83 (in a discussion of type 4 ambiguity) through the
words of Paroles (whose name means "words") — "Simply
the thing I am / Shall make me live" (*All's Well That Ends
Well* 4.3. 310–11), leaving ambiguous — double — the "thing"
he is: life and words (138).[9]

Analyzing sonnet 94 in *Some Versions of Pastoral*, Empson calculated, if not an infinitude, then the vast number
of possible meanings lodged in the relation of the four key
terms in that poem: "Taking the . . .view . . . that . . . any
one of the four is or is not and either should or should not
be like each of the others: this yields 4096 possible movements of thought, with other possibilities" (89). Faced with
this, and facing up to it, Empson takes a chance at reliev-
ing himself of the impossible burden of working through all
the possibilities by saying what he takes the poem to say; he
finds, not surprisingly, what he found in *Seven Types of Ambiguity*, that the relation between sonneteer and fair young
man is a knot that negation does not untie. W. H. is himself double (Oscar Wilde saw him as an aristocrat and a boy
actor); he embodies Empson's trick of pastoral, calling the
deprivations of the social position entailed by the "simple"
the "complexity" of the lives of those with social privilege.
This may lead ultimately to a realization that life as we are
made to live it under categories of social identity is not fully
satisfying for anyone; it may even lead to the realization that
"life is essentially inadequate to the human spirit" (114),
which is Empson's conclusion. "Success of the same nature
as yours," the sonneteer tells the young man, "is all that the
dignity, whether of life or poetry, can be based upon." Empson dubs this "queer sort of realism" (114) a "grand notion
of the inadequacy of life" (115). This conclusion about "success," like Macbeth's soliloquy, stays with an ambiguity yet
to be unraveled.

In *Seven Types of Ambiguity*, Empson abruptly concludes
his discussion of the ambiguity, "too subtle to be grasped"
in sonnet 83, by turning to offer a reading of Donne's "A
Valediction: Of Weeping." This, his longest consideration of
a poem by Donne in the book (it runs from pages 139 to 145),

puts Shakespeare in a generative position in a chapter that
arrives at Pope, Hopkins, and Wordsworth. Empson begins
to parse Donne's poem through the double grammar of the
"short middle lines" in each stanza (140), referring forward
and back, their "alternative meanings" and conjunctions:
"But *my heaven* may be in apposition to *thee*; *dissolved* may
be a participle; and *so* may be not 'in the same way' but 'so
completely, so terribly'" (142). Metaphors in the poem work
many ways; tears "may be active or passive" (141), his and
hers. She is the moon because "she is more valuable to him
than anything in the real world . . . more inconstant, or . . .
more constant" (143); the voice in the poem seems hinged
by "playfulness or brutality" (144).

As he did with Shakespeare's sonnets, Empson finally
balks at these accumulative procedures; the mind is capable of holding only so much. After that "the machinery
of interpretation . . . [becomes] too cumbrous" (145). While
the poem intimates a kind of annihilative transcendence in
the relationship between lover and beloved — "We produce
more and more tears till we drown the world altogether, and
can no longer see things like ordinary people" — it seems
also to make the beloved the agent of this double relation:
"she who has made the *world* which is his *heaven*, and she
who destroys it" (143). Although the poem seems premised
on the woman's betrayal of the man, "he almost seems to
be feeling for his hat," looking for reasons to leave (145). He
is, after all, the one parting, enjoining her to stop weeping
while he performs his imitation of her sorrow as if it were a
way to cheer them up. "But perhaps I am libeling this mas-
terpiece," Empson concludes, passing on to two other poems
by Donne that he thinks more obviously betray themselves.[10]
The holy sonnet, "What if this present were the world's last
night," does not seriously entertain the question raised, accepting with equanimity salvation paid for by "a man in the

last stages of torture" (146); the "sense of power" over the woman in "The Apparition," conveyed by "an air of detachment," is belied by "the scream of agony" (146) that reveals "an impotent desire to give any pain he can find" (147).

From Smith's perspective on metaphysical poetry, we can see that Donne's poems pose insoluble ambivalences around the couple, a minimal form of the problem of the One and the Many, the relationship between an I and an other that is already a feature of the divided I. At the beginning of his discussion of "A Valediction: Of Weeping," Empson notes that it hinges on two premises "which may not at first seem very different: . . . their love when they are together, which they must lose, is so valuable; and . . . they are 'nothing' when apart" (129). How can one be all or nothing; how can one be two? Empson ends his discussion of type 4 ambiguity by glancing at Hopkins's poem "Margaret, are you grieving"; its forward/backward motion joins consciousness and unconsciousness, "both immortality and a dolorous haunting of the grave" (149); he concludes the chapter with a consideration of Wordsworth's pantheism in which *"thought"* and *"things"* are brought together only by making *"spirit* at once intelligent and without intelligence; at once God and nature" (153). Empson can't entirely countenance this "shuffling," but also can't deny its appeal; it testifies to "a deeply rooted necessity" (154) in language, in thought, and in things, the coincidence of what is and what must be with its negation.

"An indecision and a structure, like the symbol of the Cross" (Shakespeare/Donne/Herbert)

De Man concludes his discussion of *Seven Types of Ambiguity* with a brief consideration of Herbert's "The Sacrifice" by invoking Empson's analogy for the final type of ambiguity:

"a contradiction" that "may be meaningless, but never can be blank . . . an indecision and a structure, like the symbol of the Cross" (192). The cross is a visible symbol in which opposites meet (horizontal and vertical on a grid, figure and ground, as Empson suggests). One cannot say which axis locates a place of meeting when neither axis names its point of coincidence (much the way the vanishing point in an early modern painting designates the absence upon which presence depends). As de Man writes, the reader of a poem so structured is left to (fail to?) supply "the reconciliation [that] does not occur in the text" (237). Empson moves to "The Sacrifice" by noting that "Shakespeare's use of the negative is nearly always slight and casual; he is too much interested in a word to persuade himself it is 'not' there" (206). Once again, the question is about what is there and not there at once. "One must think of the opposite of its main meaning" to think about both.

Empson takes up this crux in the final section of "Double Plots." It opens with the deifying of the beloved in Ralegh, focuses on Donne's love poems, and ends with his divine poem "The Crosse." Empson regards the symbol as "quite independent of Christianity; it is essential to man's apprehending the world" (80; it is here that he invokes James Smith's connection of metaphysical poetry to the problem of the one and the many). Donne's poem maps the world on a globe where longitude and latitude cross, declaring this meeting of "material crosses" spiritual, presumably because the globe is at once all and nothing. Donne's lines superimpose "the union of the individual to Christ or Nature"; "or" becomes "and": "Who can deny me armes, and liberty/To stretch mine armes, and my own Crosse to be?" Anyone can be in this crossed position, pulled in two directions at once across what otherwise seem impossible divides of time and space, of spirit and matter.

Donne posits a point of meeting for lovers who constitute together new worlds akin to those recently found on
this globe or hypothesized to exist elsewhere in the universe
independent of the social conditions and the institutional
forces of church and state that presume to determine earthly
lives (but that don't even extend to animals, as Marlowe's
Faustus intimates and Donne declares in Holy Sonnet 9). As
in Ralegh's "unchristian deification of Elizabeth" (73), or as
seen in statues of the Buddha at Mathura that represent him
as "the bruiser and the flower" (72), "impersonal Nature"
moots and preserves distinctions between strong and weak,
imposing and fragile. Jesus ceases to be unique; anyone can
assume his position. World-shattering, world-making lovers,
when exhumed, may be a Mary Magdalene "and I /A something else thereby"; Crashaw's weeper takes both parts (dissolution is the solution). Milton demotes God by anthropo-
morphizing, making him thereby incapable of assuming the
transcendental position in which he is necessarily the same
as the goodness he attributes to himself. "I am not sure,"
Empson continues, "how much Herbert meant by the following example,

> The bloody cross of my dear Lord
> Is both my physic and my sword." (79)

These lines from "Conscience" present the symbol in opposing aspects; the bloodiness of the cross intimates the
"common life-blood" that joins God and Nature in incarnation. "Personification . . . is incarnation" (81); metaphysics touches pantheism. In the expanse/expense of Donne's
spirit, his secret generosity borders on metempsychosis and
reincarnation; cause and effect cannot be distinguished, as
in Othello's anguished statement about "the cause," the
blood that marries him to Desdemona.

This generosity also is Empson's. He closes "Double

Plots" by recalling the lines of Chapman "about the man that joins himself to the universe" (85) that T. S. Eliot approved in "The Metaphysical Poets" and disputed in "Shakespeare and the Stoicism of Seneca": "Mr. Eliot remarked about this that no man would join himself to the universe if he had anything better to join himself to, and," Empson adds, contra Eliot but as if in agreement, "certainly there is an element of revolt in the Elizabethan use of the idea." Empson spent the rest of his career arguing for that revolt; Eliot, having declared himself joined to something better, withdrew his enthusiasm for Donne. Empson held back from holding Eliot responsible for the virulence of the neo-Christian literary criticism that he went on deploring.[11]

Empson's remarkable admission that he is "not sure how much Herbert meant" when he equated the cross as "physic" and "sword" (79) typifies his engagements with Herbert throughout *Seven Types of Ambiguity*. We got a taste of this in glancing at his discussion of categorizing "Hope" when the temporalities of repeated reading encounters change one's sense of the poem. "Hope" addresses the dilemma that Empson saw Herbert facing in every text of his that he considers, the choice between living a secular life and a spiritual one that didn't disappear even after Herbert chose to be a priest rather than a courtier, since he went on living a spiritual life as a material being. Every symbol in a Herbert poem that might seem to stand for one or the other life, Empson finds, moves in two directions at once, temporally and spatially. Herbert baffles Empson: "Shakespeare makes one accept words imaginatively; the means by which Herbert makes one accept them soberly, as things rich in their interpretations rather than in their meaning, is harder to explain in terms of syntax" (120). Empson assays an explanation in Herbert's ability to generalize; seemingly unrelated or differently located specificities are shown to be related once one abandons such categorical differences as "complex" and "simple" (121). Turning to Herbert's "The Pilgrimage," Empson responds to how much Herbert says by not saying and how the poem extends this response to us: "His readers are agog to see how much they can deduce from what he lets drop" (130). The crux (literally) hinges on the "passion" in the poem — its story about a search for a way of living allows the word to be taken "in the liturgical sense . . . about the life of renunciation," although the allegory seemed to be about "the life of ambition" (120); "After all his struggles he is only leading one of the possible good lives."

Through "The Sacrifice," the final chapter of *Seven Types of Ambiguity* makes its way in the deeply rooted univocal opposites found in a primal language that the unconscious still speaks and that can be heard in a range of authors. At the end of his book, Empson returned to the author to whom he recurs as the one who stretches him furthest: "In 'The Sacrifice,' with a magnificence he never excelled, the various sets of conflicts in the Christian doctrine of the Sacrifice are stated with an assured and easy simplicity, a reliable and assuming grandeur, extraordinary in any material, but unique as achieved by a successive fireworks of contradiction, and a mind jumping like a flea" (226). The deepest contradiction in the poem matches the final lines of "Affliction" that Empson had pondered in the previous chapter: "Ah, my dear God, though I am clean forgot,/Let me not love thee, if I love thee not" (183). The crux lies not only in the negations that go around, but in the word "love."[12] As Empson observes, Herbert puts next to each other unrelated examples and places them under seemingly knowable abstract categories (hope, passion, love, sacrifice) that he renders only more abstract by an intensity that suggests a difficulty to overcome; it "makes the poetry of George Herbert seem the product of an inner life so fully united and a belief so permanently held" (125). United permanently are tautological oppositions like the one caught in the refrain of "The Sacrifice": "Was ever grief like mine?"

"The quotation from Jeremiah . . . refers in the original not to the Saviour but to the wicked city of Jerusalem, abandoned by God, and in the hands of her enemies" (227), Empson notes. Lamentations 1:12 reads, "Is it nothing to you, all ye that pass by? Behold, and see if there be any sorrow like unto my sorrow, which is done unto me, wherewith the Lord hath afflicted me in the day of his fierce anger." The "I" of the poem is singular and plural, male and female, savior and sinner.[13] The one lamenting is the one condemning. Empson glimpses a similar scene in Crashaw's poem, "Luke xi. Blessed be the paps that thou hast sucked," in which Mary suckling the babe does not feed his hunger for the blood she will ultimately suck from his wound: "The sacrificial idea is aligned with incest, the infantile pleasures, and cannibalism; we contemplate the god with a sort of savage chuckle; he is made to flower, a monstrous hermaphrodite deity, in the glare of short-circuiting the human order" (221).

In the 1950s Empson was drawn to quarrel with Helen Gardner's editing of Donne and into a long exchange with Rosemond Tuve about "The Sacrifice."[14] Tuve and Empson came to see that they saw the same thing in the poem. Tuve appreciated what Empson emphasized, Herbert's "connexions" that "reawaken into new life whole complexes of meaning, deeper, more ancient and more inclusive than the meanings any man's single experience can provide."[15] For her, he erred only by supposing that Herbert invented contradictions she documents in liturgical texts and popular hymns, all related in one way or another to Lamentations. Empson is aghast at the threats uttered in a poem spoken by a supposedly loving deity who sacrificed himself for all of

us. Tuve counters: "The instrument of irony which brings
in overtones of terrible pathos when used to lay bare the
nature of ingratitude operates differently when it is used to
point to the sin of hubris. It becomes then cruel as a knife,
and the overtones are tones of terror. A dominant theme
in the whole poem is the sureness of justice to come; it is
not *sotto voce* as Empson reads it, borne in on the possible
connotations of ambiguous phrases, but as clear and awful
as the *Dies irae*" (74). Humanity is punished; God's chosen
beloved, the city of Jerusalem, type of the mother Church,
is condemned of ingratitude for not accepting the sacrifice.
Tuve's "ingratitude" could be uttered by Milton's God, who
calls us "ingrate" (*PL* 3.97) for choosing to eat the apple and
exercise the free will we were given to misuse. Justice, Tuve
calls it, as does Milton's God when he calls for a victim:
"Die he or justice must" (*PL* 3.210). Empson is sure that
"Herbert was far more conscious of the monstrosity" of this
(as he thought that Milton was, too).[16] When Tuve contemplates "the heart of the Mystery" (41), she can see a "joker"
(49). Empson's outrage at the scenario — climbing the cross,
Jesus replaces the apple — Tuve accepts as a commonplace
identification.

Empson ends his analysis with lines spoken by Jesus as the
replacement of the forbidden fruit: "Alas! What have I stolen from you? Death: /Was ever grief like mine?" Christ has
stolen death; he dies and is resurrected. We die and won't re-
gain bodily existence until there is no time. We were warned
not to eat the apple without knowing the meaning of the
word we needed to know; "death" was not in our vocabulary.
Everything that existed always would, it seemed. In *Paradise
Lost* God and Son enjoy jokes, punning at our expense; so
too does Satan, the son who never dies so long as we do (he
is made responsible for death so that God is not). Satan sets
off fireworks in the war in heaven; to Empson, they illustrate

"the interaction between separated parts of the mind" (102).
Herbert brought them together in "The Sacrifice."

Marvell's Garden: The Ideal Simplicity
Approached by Resolving Contradictions

De Man concludes his discussion of Empson by glancing at
Some Versions of Pastoral to claim that in it Empson shows
"that the pastoral theme is, in fact, the only poetic theme"
(239), "poetic consciousness as an essentially divided, sor-
rowful, and tragic consciousness" (241). Singling out Empson's chapter, "Marvell's "Garden: *The Ideal Simplicity Approached by Resolving Contradiction*," he focuses on lines
from the sixth stanza, "Annihilating all that's made / To a
green thought in a green shade" (47–48), to demonstrate
"the essentially negative activity of all thought . . . , and poetic thought in particular" (238). Annihilation of the green
world is recouped doubly in the activity of mind and the image it produces; this illustrates "the contradictory relations
between natural being and the being of consciousness."
"What is the pastoral convention," he asks, "if not the eternal
separation between the mind that distinguishes, negates, leg-
islates, and the originary simplicity of the natural?" (239). De
Man's distinction sounds rather like James Smith's between
noumenon and phenomenon that Empson answered. As de
Man acknowledges, Empson grapples with the contradictory "intuition of oneness with an object and his intuition
of the object's otherness" (243). He does that not to further
de Man's distinctions, but as he says toward the end of his
essay, by suggesting how Marvell's poem offers "a more and
more inclusive account of the mind's relation to Nature"
(145). Inclusiveness is Empson's goal too in exploring "the
contradictory relations between natural being and the being of consciousness" that de Man takes to be his subject

(239). These ontological questions are the crux of the poem. Through mind and nature it asks (Empson asks of it) the question of the relation of human existence to what is.

Empson begins by looking at the lines de Man cites, finding in them "a crucial double meaning . . . about the Mind"; these lines guide Empson's analysis in the first half of his chapter. As he did with the Arden edition of Shakespeare, Empson finds authority for what he makes of them in a scholarly apparatus, this time in the note to them in H. M. Margoliouth's standard Oxford edition of Marvell.[17] "So this at least is not my own fancy," Empson wryly comments (119). Margoliouth says that the lines "Annihilating all that's made / To a green Thought" "may be taken as meaning either 'reducing the whole material world to nothing material, i.e., to a green thought,' or 'considering the whole material world as of no value compared to a green thought'" (226). Empson heightens the contradiction by restating this double meaning as "either contemplating everything or shutting everything out" (119). Empson's "or" means "and"; de Man takes Empson's allusion to the "humble, permanent, undeveloped nature which sustains everything, and to which everything must return," as Empson puts it (128) as a reference to something lost. Empson's words posit an existence that overcomes absolute separation in the ambiguity of being.

Empson redistributes (crosses) what is negated (shut out) and what is recovered (let in) by seeing both as activities of the mind. The "conscious mind" can include everything because it is capable of understanding; it is doubled by "the unconscious animal nature, including everything because in harmony with it"; human being is inseparable from material being, from an animality it shares with nature ("animal" derives from "anima," soul, life, motion). The mind turned two ways offers "nothing" and thought, nothing but thought; as Empson continues, the unconscious mind is also the "primitive" (120) mind magically believing that it creates what is. For de Man, language creates what is; through it we conceive reality. Empson, having posited the mind as intellectual and conscious and as unconscious, primitive, and magical, comes to an astounding conclusion: "The point is not that these two are essentially different but that they must cease to be different so far as either can be known" (119).

Empson reconciles what de Man separates without denying the difference he attempts to overcome. His thought could not be denser; these questions recur as attempts to grasp how the unthinkable — the unthought — can be thought or can be in the mind even as it remains unthought. To come to think the difference between those categories one must first grapple with the original simplicity in which they are no different. Empson's object is not nature per se or the mind per se, but their relation in Marvell's poem. It is a real relation.[18] Empson italicizes "to" to emphasize that the preposition does double duty. Two meanings of "to" produce the crucial double meaning in these lines.

Several pages later, after glancing at the opening and closing of "The Garden," Empson returns to "the crisis of the poem . . . in the middle" (124): "Once you accept this note" (Margoliouth's), he counsels, "you may as well apply it to the whole verse." He backtracks to the opening of stanza six in which "The Mind . . .Withdraws into its happiness" "from pleasure less"; mind enters itself, either thanks to the lesser pleasures of country life that promote an increase in intellectual acuity or thanks to the effects of country pleasures to relax mental activity to promote a "mind less worrying and introspective" (125). "This is the same paradox as to the consciousness of thought," Empson contends, and "the same doubt gives all its grandeur to the next lines." In question is the relationship between the "repose" and "release" of consciousness, its lessening and heightening. The prefix "re-" hints at the doubt — the dubious doubling — of the paradoxical happiness achieved, a happenstance nonetheless actively sought. "Re-" conveys repetition, of course, but also attaches to "res," "rem," to things, and to "rien," the nothing tied etymologically to them; it points the way ahead and the way back, preserving and erasing the distinction.

"Reflect" is a word for this and for the correspondence theory of knowledge proposed when "The Mind" is described as an "Ocean where each kind / Does streight its own resemblance find" (42–43); sea-horses and sea-lions (Empson's examples) mirror the land creatures that name them. At the same time, however, the sea is fathomless like the mind. One mirror dwells in resemblances that are shadows, the other in solidities akin to green thoughts, fathomable only insofar as the adjective "green" insists on a reality that can be visible; it holds the possibility of the "pure knowledge" housed in the "fantastic echo" of imagined correspondence. Reflection is double: subject and object coincide without being identical. "This metaphor" (of resemblance) may "reflect back" on "*withdraws*," Empson continues, so that "it may mean either "'withdraws into self-contemplation' or 'withdraws altogether, into its mysterious processes of digestion'" (125–26). These double meanings of mental and physical activity (along with a glance at a Freudian return to the womb in an oceanic experience of tidal flow) describe at once an encounter with what is and with what the mind makes. They are found in "streight," a word that could mean tightly packed together, or all at once. Spatial/temporal doubling leads Empson to recall the stanzas of the poem he had considered before his return to the crucial ones, those that take "up a large part of its overt thought" (126), "entrancingly witty verses about the sublimation of sexual desire into a taste for Nature." What would it mean if all our desires were forms of a desire for nature? The serious wit of the poem "implies self-consciousness and all the antinomies of philosophy" (126); this "sublimation" (both an elevation and an abjection) leads Empson to another staggering formulation: "In including everything in itself the mind includes as a detail itself and all its inclusions" (126). Empson's inclusiveness looks like an Escher drawing or a hologram, a mirror whose comprehensiveness includes itself as a detail in something that exceeds itself even in withdrawing into itself. There is no itself in the singular.

"All the *kinds* look for their *resemblance*, in practice, out of a desire for *creation*" (126), Empson italicizes, tracing the correspondences between the created world and the poet's. The metaphor of mind as ocean implicates that oceanic quality in the mental activity that the poem describes and replicates (in itself, in us). The ocean, Empson writes, "reflects the *other worlds* of the stars." The sea also has its kraken: "In the depths as well as the transcendence of the mind are things stranger than all the kinds of the world" (126). Our minds are not estranged from the strangeness of what is but what is in it.

Empson spends several pages exploring the recurrence of "green" across Marvell's oeuvre, pausing for a paragraph before he does that to consider stanza vii and M. C. Bradbrook on its religious meaning.[19] He follows her suggestion that the bird in this stanza is the Holy Spirit (and the dove of the Covenant); an image of a transported, transcendent creative capacity, "in becoming everything," it is in two places at once, "above and apart from the world even while living in it." Transcendence coincides with imminence; the life of the mind and soul may transport us as if out of body, but we nonetheless remain embodied. The bird on the bough is a bird *in* the bough. The bird is a figure, a simile, its natural life one with its life in the poem. "The paradoxes are still firmly maintained here, and the soul is as solid as the green thought" (127), providing yet another instance of the "penetrating theory" of the sixth stanza, he remarks.

Moving ahead, Empson turns back to the fifth stanza to insist on the thought found in it that has been ignored in the usual appreciations of it as "the only poetical verse of the poem" (131). "What wond'rous Life in this I lead" (33), stanza five opens. The "Alpha and Omega of that life," Empson notes, is "the Apple and the Fall" (133). As in stanza vii, Christian imagery does not displace the terms of the "praise of solitude" central to the poem (132). This garden gives itself to him and ensnares him as well; his "repose" in it figures what it means to be "contemplating *all that's made*" (Empson italicizes), an embodied thought process that also is an exercise in "sensibility" (132). Empson likens the experience here to Milton's Garden. The double life of mind and body, within oneself and in the world, redoubles in the "mean while" (41) of the sixth stanza: "It is while this is going on . . . that the mind performs its ambiguous and memorable *withdrawal*. For each of the three central verses he gives a twist to the screw of the microscope and he is living in another world" (132).[20] That "other world" is nonetheless our world; it also is what the poem is. To live the life of the mind is to live a double life.

"I must go back to the *annihilating* lines," Empson opens the next paragraph, but, in fact, he has finished his reading of them in the first half of his essay. In leaving that task behind, Empson has nonetheless provided us a language for further analysis; "*annihilating* lines" of thought continue: to turn everything into nothing — and into thought — difference must "cease to be different in order for it to be known" (119). "Repose" in the garden fulfills "one's powers" (130). This is the frame of the poem, from men's search for fame (as generals, politicians, and poets) in the first stanza

to the floral homage that leads to its echo in the "grace-
ful finale" (124) of the final stanza in which human activity
is compared to bee pollination. "'Women, I am pleased to
say, are no longer interesting to me, because nature is more
beautiful'" (130–31), Empson crassly paraphrases the sublimation theme, the climax of the argument of the poem. He
proceeds to rethink this "witty" conclusion by way of the
"truth-seeking idea . . . fundamental to the European convention of love-poetry" (135).

To trace the line of thought that leads there, we need to
retrace quickly Empson's earlier handling of the "violence
of the couplet" about annihilation; it offers a "hint of physical power in thought itself" that enables it to overcome
the force of nature (120), Empson contends, and is found
in Romantic poetry (Smart, Coleridge, and Byron provide
examples). Submission to nature is the way to overcome it
("by delight in Nature when terrible man gains strength to
control it" 120); this chimes with the sexual "sublimation"
Empson goes on to find in "The Garden." "Masculine energy . . . balanced immediately by an acceptance of Nature
more masochist than passive"; so Empson describes a moment of entanglement in briar in "Upon Appleton House"
that he links to the "repose" of "The Garden." So, too, in
stanza five, "the triumph of the sexual interest upon nature"
comes when the "eatable beauties give themselves so as to
lose themselves, like a lover" who submits to ensnare (132).
Active and passive cross in masochistic desire. Compared to
"pleasure," "happiness" is, as a rule, a "weak" word, Empson
contends; but in Marvell's lines about the mind's withdrawal
"the verse makes it act as a strong one" (125).

Empson deploys "strong" and "weak" in all-too-familiar
terms of gender difference, but also reverses them, bringing
them into proximity through his annihilating notion that
difference only can be known by way of non-difference. To

know gender difference one must think the genders' sameness; to happily renounce women for garden love is a route to
doing this. It's articulated in the penultimate stanza of "The
Garden," at which Empson barely glances, curiously not
citing the closing couplet: "Two Paradises 'twere in one / To
live in Paradise alone" (64–65). Nonetheless, two-in-oneness
centers Empson's ontological query; it's the fundamental
property of ambiguity and of the "trick" of pastoral.

Empson explores the truth of that plot in love poetry of
the West: first, in several pages on Donne, concentrating on
"The Extasie," then through some lines from the exchange
of Touchstone and Audrey in *As You Like It*. Donne joins
lovers, at first in a disembodied communion of souls (a "dialogue of one," 74) enjoined to physical union. "Spirit," the
word for their first form of union, "sense" for the second,
can both mean both states. Donne may be articulating a
cynical speaker's desire for sex ("Else a great Prince in
prison lies," 68), but Empson also insists that he must have
believed his elevated metaphysical claims. Spirits are vital
physical forces as well as animate beings of a middle nature
(Empson hammers this point on spirits in his later work on
Shakespeare).[21] The sexual/sensual meanings of "sense" do
not limit the word. Soul and body are "interfused" (133).
Donne's vocabulary comes from current philosophy and
goes back to the "genuine primitive use" of language that
Empson identified at the end of *Seven Types of Ambiguity*.
His poetry takes part in a tradition in which "love is . . . idealized as a source of knowledge not only of the other party
but of oneself and of the world" (135).

"Personalized Nature is treated both as external to man
and as created by the instinct of the mind, and by tricks
of language these are made to seem the same" (136). The
"ideal simplicity" in "The Garden" resolves the differences
between Mind and Nature, Man and Woman: "What we

feel is that though they are essentially unlike they are practically unlike in different degrees at different times; a supreme condition can therefore be imagined, though not attained, in which they are essentially like" (136). What is unattainable here and now is the realization of what the mind attempts to grasp that is beyond the limits of consciousness to know. "A hint of the supreme condition is thus found in the actual one (this makes the actual one include everything in itself)" (136).

At this point Empson turns to Shakespeare to confirm his argument; a pun on fain/feign vehiculates it. Touchstone wishes that Audrey might be "poetical" (3.3.14), by which he means that in professing her honesty, Audrey only be pretending to refuse his sexual advances.

Once again, the situation involves a knowing cynicism about the language of seduction: "The root of the joke is that a physical desire drives the human creature to a spiritual one" (138). But, as Empson immediately, wittily, continues, "To write poetry is not the quickest way to satisfy desire; there must be some other impulse behind the convention of love-poetry; something feigned in the choice of topic; some other thing of which they are fain." Empson's point is hardly his invention: Plato's *Symposium* or *Phaedrus* and all the texts that follow its explorations of the nature of love lead to the conclusion that the expression of desire, while never precluding a sexual impetus, aims at "some other thing," often at some originary state of union with something other than but nonetheless constitutive of one's desire, "levels mysteriously inter-related which a sane man separates only for a joke" (138). Empson adverts here once again to James Smith's theorization of metaphysical wit, casting this now as an Aristotelian quandary about form and matter (139), recasting it as the relation of "the One and the Many" a few pages later (142). "Two ideas are united which in normal use are contradictory, and our machinery of interpretation so acts that we feel there is a series of senses in which they could be more and more truly combined" (139). Metaphysical wit is not just a matter of jokes and puzzles; Empson hopes that Smith recognizes "on his account a metaphysical conceit is essentially a vivid statement of a puzzle, and in practice it is more" (140). This reminder, directed at Smith, who, Empson concedes, probably doesn't need it, may as easily be a reminder to himself that slighting the erotic aspect of "The Garden" in favor of its penetrating theory may also answer to that charge. So might "penetrating."

The dialogue between Touchstone and Audrey emblematizes the pastoral assumption "that you can say everything about complex people by a complete consideration of simple people" (137). Touchstone is a courtly clown pretending to be simple; Audrey is a rustic, supposedly easily duped. "Complex" and "simple" share the same etymological root in their endings; "-ple" is a join, as in "plait," a braid; "com-" and "sim-" both imply coming together as one. Weaving the garlands of repose, Empson chose "resolve" as the word in the subtitle of his essay to describe the coming-together broached in "The Garden," resolving a solution by dissolving it; "re-" repeats and negates what it brings together.

"What machinery erects a staircase on a contradiction?"

As if responding to de Man's claim that pastoral "is poetry itself," "an ontology of the poetic" (239), Empson concludes his essay on "The Garden" by invoking as "the fountainhead of simplicity" quite another text, Homer's epic, but to show how its complexity answers to that description. The lives of Homeric heroes depend on social rules that include a satisfaction in all aspects of life: "Ajax is still enormously grand when he cooks his dinner" (141); heroic male gran-

deur (including the war for "detested Helen" [142]) bears
the marks of pastoral humility. If "'no one . . . knows how to
live the ideal [it] is easily reached'" by Homer's heroes, who
embody what Empson dubs the "inspiriting moral paradox"
that epic poetry shares with pastoral.

It is symbolized in the relation of heroes to gods, humans
to immortals. It raises a central philosophical "puzzle about
how far men can be free." Empson ventures that Homer's
gods may represent "forces in their minds"; that is suggested
when Homer marks with a "but" Minerva's indifference to
the fate she pronounces, as if she were mouthing a human
thought (142). More modern versions of Homeric materials, like Shakespeare's *Troilus and Cressida* (a central text
for "Double Plots"), "often taken as a sort of parody of the
Iliad" (143), pick up on Homer's notion of simplicity. Both
as a critic of Homer and in "the strange world" he creates for
Adam, Milton does, too.

"What machinery erects a staircase on a contradiction"?:
this question arises; Empson finds himself unable to answer
it. He attempts to do so by laying out a linguistic premise
that underlies his poetics: "Any statement of identity between terms already defined ('God is love') is a contradiction because you already know they are not identical" (143).
The ontological problem lies in the verb "is" that posits an
identity. In the example "God is love," the "traffic rule"
(144) of predication explains how identity contradicts itself.
It's obvious that subject and predicate are in a hierarchical
relation if you reverse the sentence to "Love is God." The
case of "Might is Right" vs. "Right is Might" is not so simple,
and Empson takes a page to work out some possible expla-
nations of how "other uses than the expression of identity"
can be found in "is" (144). By "shifting the words again and
again" interpretation can be made to produce a unity, but
not an identity; words can't be made to mean "the same"

when reassembled "like parts of an organism" (145). Their
life remains contradictory, in motion, intractable.

"The seventh Buddhist state of enlightenment"

Empson ends his essay by returning to claims in its opening
paragraph that we have yet to notice (like the opening sentence of the essay, they baffle the reader). From Homeric
quandaries of fate and free will Empson follows the legacy of
Greece: "When it arrived in India," he notes, it bore "none
of the interest in the problems of free-will; the dignity of the
heroes of the Mahabharata is based on puzzles about the
One and the Many" (142); once again the philosophic term
that Empson took from James Smith's analysis of the metaphysics of metaphysical poetry recurs. Empson continues
his point by alluding to a story about the Buddha brush-
ing aside the fate/free will quandary: "I understand that all
Buddhist theologians have ignored the issue" (142). Ending
here, we are brought back to the opening claim of the essay:
"The chief point of the poem is to contrast and reconcile
conscious and unconscious states, intuitive and intellectual
modes of apprehension; and yet that distinction is never
made, perhaps could not have been made; his thought is im-
plied by his metaphors. There is something very Far-Eastern
about this" (119). Empson's final move recalls his opening
gambit: "I was set to work on the poem by Dr. Richards'
recent discussion of a philosophical argument in Mencius"
(119), he continues, breaking off his opening train of thought
to open the one we, with him, first pursued by way of the Oxford note on the "double meaning" in "the most analytical
statement of the poem about the Mind."[22]

Empson refers to "Human Nature: An Early Chinese Argument" where Richards states that he only can formulate
the argument in Mencius through terms Mencius does not

deploy because Eastern thought fails to provide the fine logical distinctions upon which Western rationality depends.
What something is and what a word means are confused
in Mencius. (It was this distinction that de Man faulted
in Richards as the basis of Empson's distance from him.)
"From the point of view of Western logic," Richards writes
(68), Mencius is lacking. "Distinctions, none of which show
at all in Mencius' language, are highly relevant to the argument" (64), those between the particular and the general,
between words and things, between human nature and nature in general. All get collapsed in an indistinct singularity
called "life." Mencius depends on analogy, but "the critical
development of the analogy that is most natural to us was
one which *never* occurs in Chinese discussion"; hence,
there is a complete failure of "analytic logic" (69).

Empson pursues as thought what Richards could only
term "poetic" (76), not what he thought philosophic thought
should be. Empson aims to bring East and West together,
as did Richards. He asks the question Richards poses, what
"hierarchy of possible developments . . . can be erected"
(69), what "machinery" explains "the psychology" of the
argument in Mencius, what "incidental steps" perform the
"ambitious metaphysical undertakings" of abstraction that
lead from the specific to the general, the word to the thing
(71). Empson may not finally answer this question, no more
than he could definitively answer Smith's about the phe-
nomenal and the noumenal. "I have not been able to say
what machinery erects a staircase on a contradiction," Empson writes toward the conclusion of his essay, "but then the
only essential for the poet is to give the reader a chance to
build an interesting one" (143).

One other gesture eastward appears close to the conclusion of Empson's opening paragraph on "The Garden":
"So far as he has achieved his state of ecstasy he combines

them, he is 'neither conscious nor not conscious,' like the
seventh Buddhist state of enlightenment" (119–20). Empson
presumably alludes here to the noble eightfold path; its seventh stage involves mindfulness. Charles Eliot, a historian
of Eastern thought whom Empson cites frequently in the
section on theology in *The Faces of the Buddha*, notes that
all of the stages involve intense mental activity.[23] Thanissaro
Bhikkhu offers this translation of an early authoritative Pali
text on the seventh state, "right mindfulness"; it involves focus on "the body in & of itself," "on feelings in & of themselves," "on the mind in & of itself," "on mental qualities
in & of themselves."[24] These match the range in Marvell's
poem, although the description of the final stage of concentration that follows sounds even closer to what Empson calls
the seventh stage; it involves "withdrawal" from sensuality
at the same time as entering and remaining in a state of
"rapture & pleasure." "Directed thought and evaluation"
continue in this stage, along with further acts of withdrawal
of consciousness. Those final steps can be approached in
life, but also can be imagined as achieved beyond life, or in
death. To whom, when, and how this happens is only further
complicated by Buddhist theories of impersonality. Eliot
summarizes a crux when he notes that "though the Buddha
denied that there is in man anything permanent that can
be called the self, this does not imply a denial that human
nature can by mental training be changed into something
different, something infinitely superior to the nature of the
ordinary man" (1:219–20). Of this state, in phrases that seem
akin to Empson's "neither nor," but that go even further,
Eliot reports a story of how the Buddha told a disciple that
"it does not fit the case to say either that he is reborn, not
reborn, both reborn and not reborn, or neither reborn nor
not reborn" (1:231). Empson cites this passage in *The Faces of
the Buddha*, his book on how asymmetrical representations

of the Buddha's face produce an effect of humanization by combining absolute withdrawal with availability.

Eliot concludes his discussion of the eightfold path by attending to the metaphors through which is presented what happens as self approaches its annihilation. It is like a particular fire being extinguished (which does not mean there is no longer any fire), or a wave finally dissolving and becoming indistinguishable from the ocean (which does not mean there won't be any more waves). "All form by which one could predicate the existence of the saint [in the translation of the Pali text for enlightened human beings (Arhats) that Eliot cites] is abandoned and uprooted" (1:231). Eliot comments, "Nirvana is the cessation of a process not the annihilation of an existence. If I take a walk, nothing is annihilated when the walk comes to an end: a particular form of action has ceased" (1:232). So too with a fire or a wave. This is not to say that in its cessation, the form persists: "The saint who is released from what is styled form is deep, immeasurable, hard to fathom, like the great ocean" (1:231). Or, as Marvell has it, transcending resemblance, the mind annihilates all that's made "To a green thought in a green shade."

Empson maintains the vagueness Smith faulted in his review of *Seven Types of Ambiguity*: "This talk about a hierarchy of 'levels' is vague I can cheerfully admit," he opens the final paragraph of his essay on "The Garden." Perhaps the Buddhist notion of "dependent arising," the claim that everything is related to everything else, attracted Empson. Empson's essay takes off from "The Garden" on a path of thought that leads away from it and returns to it to close, perhaps in part out of the belief that metaphysical poetry in general deals with fundamental philosophical truths, certainly because, as he says in his final sentence, "only a metaphysical poet with so perfect a sense of form and so complete a control over the tricks of the style, at the end of its development, could actually dramatise these hints as he gave them" (145). If "to find your way into the interpretation seems essentially a process of shifting the words again and again" (145), the essence thereby is anything but essential; nothing is permanent, and everything is related. Empson specifies this through a final summary of the three stanzas in Marvell's poem that have preoccupied him, its gist delivered in hints. "But the three central verses of the Marvell poem are at least a definite example: in the course of suggesting various interlocking hierarchies (knowing that you know that you know, reconciling the remaining unconscious with the increasing consciousness, uniting in various degrees perception and creation, the one and the many), it does in fact rise through a hierarchy of three sharply contrasted styles and with them give a more and more inclusive account of the mind's relation to Nature" (145). "An idea that you must be somehow satisfied as well as mortified before entering repose goes deep into the system, and perhaps into human life." So Empson writes, not, as it happens, on repose in "The Garden," but in a version of "The Faces of Buddha" published in 1936, a year after *Some Versions of Pastoral* first appeared.[25]

Acknowledgments

I am very glad to be published again by Fordham University Press. My thanks to Richard Morrison for taking an interest in this book, to Tom Lay for once again seeing a book of mine through the editing process with aplomb and care (and thanks to the two anonymous readers he chose who recommended the book for publication); thanks again to Eric Newman for guiding my book through publication, and to Aldene Fredenburg for welcome light copyediting. I am grateful to Laurie Shannon for allowing me to use one of her wonderful photographs for the cover of this book, and not for that alone. Laurie is among my dearest and closest distant friends who have been with me during these last difficult years as I completed work on this book. Those others include Marcie Frank, Sharon Cameron, and Karen Newman; their friendship sustains me. Hal Rogers continues to lend me invaluable support, for which I am grateful. Dan Kirslis and Kylie Woodall are always welcome to J&M's Bistro. Michael Moon has been the sole reader of this book in all its many revisions, and once again always has supported me in this and in every other way. My love for him knows no limits. It has been quite a while since I last acknowledged my daughters, Julia and Abigail; it certainly is time to do that again now.

Notes

Introduction

1. Virginia Woolf, *Mr. Bennett and Mrs. Brown* (London: Hogarth, 1924), 4.

2. Christopher Hilliard, *English as a Vocation: The* Scrutiny *Movement* (Oxford: Oxford University Press, 2012), 25, notes that as early as *New Bearings in English Poetry* (1932), Leavis "was a powerful advocate for the work performed by Eliot's rereading . . . of Jacobean literature." Francis Mulhern, *The Moment of "Scrutiny"* (London: NLB, 1979), 135, emphasizes that "the literature of late-sixteenth- and seventeenth-century England was *Scrutiny's* most constant interest." These early efforts were succeeded in the transatlantic professional development of the canon in which the antithesis between Donne and Milton joined another split between the methodology of close reading vs. historicization that defined the field, up to the New Historicism, that ventured to do both; significantly, that methodology was first launched around early modern texts.

3. T. S. Eliot, *Selected Essays* (London: Faber and Faber, 1951), 289.

4. Giorgio Agamben, *The Fire and the Tale*, trans. Lorenzo Chiasa (Stanford: Stanford University Press, 2014), 34.

5. The sentence is underlined by Eliot in his annotated copy of *De Anima*; it is in The Papers of the Hayward Bequest (HB/B/2). I am grateful to Ronald Schuchard for putting me in touch with Claire Reihill, a trustee of Eliot's estate; she in turn authorized Peter Monteith, the archivist at Cambridge Kings, to send me copies of the text.

6. Woolf met Eliot in 1918 and quickly became a close friend, as numerous diary entries and letters reveal; her hesitations about his poetry registered there also can be found in *Mr. Bennet and Mrs. Brown*. Her response to his criticism is not easily summarized categorically, for while the absence of women writers from it was something she sought to remedy, many of Eliot's premises about artistic creation resonate with Woolf's. One instance of this double-mindedness: she faults Eliot's poems for the difficulty of their connections, implying in them the lack of an objective correlative he considered necessary to make literature something other than personal confession (or withholding).

7. Virginia Woolf, *A Room of One's Own* (Orlando: Harcourt, 1929, 2005), 112.

8. Rachel Cusk, in "Shakespeare's Sisters," in *Coventry* (New York: Farrar, Straus and Giroux, 2019), 163–76, interrogates Woolf's claims and agendas for the woman writer.

9. The complex relations between the homosocial, the homoerotic, and the homophobic were early explored in Eve Kosofsky Sedgwick, *Between Men: English Literature and Male Homosocial Desire* (New York: Columbia University Press, 1985). In *Epistemology of the Closet* (Berkeley: University of California Press, 1990), Sedgwick's parsing of universalizing and minoritizing definitions of sexuality and the gender separatisms and crossings involved speak to the complexity of cross-categorical thinking; see 27–35 for her succinct theorization.

10. Virginia Woolf, *Moments of Being*, ed Jeanne Schulkind (San Diego: Harcourt Brace, 1985), 72.

11. William Empson, "The Style of the Master," first appeared in Richard March and Tambimuttu, eds., *T. S. Eliot: A Symposium*; I cite from its reprinting in *Argufying*, ed. John Haffenden (Iowa City: University of Iowa Press, 1987), 361.

12. See Michael Wood, *On Empson* (Princeton: Princeton University Press, 2017), 9.

13. William Empson, *Seven Types of Ambiguity* (New York: New Directions, 1947), 196. Throughout I cite from this second edition of the book; it first appeared in 1930.

14. James Smith, "On Metaphysical Poetry," *Scrutiny* 2, no. 3 (December 1933): 227.

15. Empson, *Seven Types of Ambiguity*, 131–32. Empson here is siding with I. A. Richards against Eliot. In "The Active Universe," *Critical Quarterly* 5, no. 3 (Sept. 1963): 267–71, Empson revisits the prejudices about Shelley, Romantic poetry, and pantheism that he shared — and disputed — with Eliot as he reviews arguments by H. W. Piper that align the liveness of inanimate matter in nineteenth-century science and poetry with early modern beliefs in a spirit-inhabited nature. "'Shelley,' says Mr. Piper, 'continued to believe that the cause of mind is unlike mind'" (270). Empson stayed with the inhuman/human ambiguity of life.

In a review of a new translation of Ernst Cassirer's *Philosophy of Symbolic Forms*, "The Symbolic Animal," *New York Review of Books* 68, no. 6 (April 8, 2021), Adam Kirsch remarks on the possibility that the philosopher whose Kantianism seemed to make him a relic after Heidegger might yet have something to say, taking as an example Cassirer's attachment to the thinking he found in so-called primitive languages (espoused as foundational by Empson). "Some African and Australian languages," Kirsch summarizes Cassirer's argument, "have numbers for one and two but refer to all higher quantities simply as 'many.'" The explanation of this? One and two recognize that there is an I and a you, separate entities with "separate minds. . . . It took a further conceptual leap to refer to 'he' and 'she' — the third person for which the number three was required," and for the particular to be generalized (53).

16. William Empson, *Some Versions of Pastoral* (London: Chatto and Windus, 1950), 119.

17. Helen Thaventhiran, *Radical Empiricists: Five Modernist Close Readers* (Oxford: Oxford University Press, 2015). Thaventhiran is one of the editors, with Stefan Collini, of a new annotated edition of *The Structure of Complex Words* (Oxford: Oxford University Press, 2020).

18. Joseph North, *Literary Criticism: A Concise Political History* (Cambridge, Mass.: Harvard University Press, 2017), 213–15. North shares the determinate story of John Guillory, "The Ideology of Canon-Formation: T. S. Eliot and Cleanth Brooks," *Critical Inquiry* 10, no. 1 (September 1983): 173–98.

19. Cleanth Brooks, *The Well Wrought Urn* (New York: Harcourt, Brace & World, 1947), 9. Tristram Woolf, "That's Close Enough: The Unfinished History of Emotivism in Close Reading," *PMLA* 134, no. 1 (January 2019): 51–65, assumes that Richards is the father of New Criticism and its attempts to separate meaning from the taint of emotion, a version of De Man's critique of Richards.

20. Jem Bloomfield, "Mid-Century Jacobeans: Agatha Christie, Ngaio Marsh, P. D. James, and the *Duchess of Malfi*," *ELH* 87, no. 4 (Winter 2020): 1,079–1,104.

21. Simon During, "When Literary Criticism Mattered," in Rónán McDonald, ed., *The Value of Literary Studies* (Cambridge: Cambridge University Press, 2015), 136. During further contextualizes Leavis's practices in "Exciting Discipline," *Australian Humanities Review* 68 (May 2021): 59–63, his contribution to a forum in that issue led off by William Christie, "'The Essential Cambridge in Spite of Cambridge': F. R. Leavis in the Antipodes," 1–15; Christie opens by noting that Richards was "the thinker arguably responsible for the motivating principle of Leavis's criticism" (1). As he details, the principle may have involved "collaboration and the common pursuit" of "life," but it was "intolerant of any disagreement" (7). In his contribution to the forum, Kevin Pask, "Resistance to Teaching," 38–41, effectively disputes the claim that Richards's teaching of literary

judgment was collaborative; he characterizes it rather as entailing "public shaming" (39) of students who failed to deliver correct judgments based in socially policed notions of correct meaning. Early modern literature modeled how texts were to be handled (40) to deliver these judgments, a point also glanced at by Christie (4).

22. Simon During, "The Philosophical Origins of Modern Literary Criticism," on the Academia.edu website. Ann Banfield likewise situates the aesthetics of Woolf and Fry in Cambridge philosophy in *The Phantom Table: Woolf, Fry, Russell, and the Epistemology of Modernism* (New York: Cambridge University Press, 2000). See also her chapter on "Cambridge Bloomsbury," in Victoria Rosner, ed., *The Cambridge Companion to the Bloomsbury Group* (Cambridge: Cambridge University Press, 2014).

23. These classical and modern strands of philosophical thought join in Giorgio Agamben, *Potentialities* (Stanford: Stanford University Press, 1999). Brett Defries, "'Whatsoever Being': Agamben, Donne, and Lovability," *ELH* 85, no. 2 (Summer 2018): 415–40, posits an ontological link between being lovable in Donne and Agamben's "whatever-being," "being-thus": "The being of the worm, Agamben all too perfectly says, 'is divine'" (429).

24. See Steven Matthews, *T. S. Eliot and Early Modern Literature* (Oxford: Oxford University Press, 2013); Alice Fox, *Virginia Woolf and the Literature of the English Renaissance* (Oxford: Clarendon, 1990). Juliet Dusinberre, *Virginia Woolf's Renaissance: Woman Reader or Common Reader?* (Iowa City: University of Iowa Press, 1997) does include some discussion of Woolf's criticism, always with an eye to how it advances her feminism; Sally Greene, ed., *Virginia Woolf Reading the Renaissance* (Athens: Ohio University Press, 1999), collects essays almost all of which are about Shakespeare allusions in Woolf's novels. One exception is David McWhirter, "Woolf, Eliot, and the Elizabethans: The Politics of Modernist Nostalgia," in Greene, *Virginia Woolf Reading the Renaissance*, 245–66. Beth

Carole Rosenberg and Jeanne Dubino, eds., *Virginia Woolf and the Essay* (N.Y.: St. Martin's, 1997) surveys the context and content of the essays; Sally Greene, "Entering Woolf's Renaissance Imaginary: A Second Look at *The Second Common Reader*," in Rosenberg and Dubino, *Virginia Woolf and the Essay*, 81–95, usefully focuses on the early modern essays for that volume in an argument that counters then prevailing claims that Woolf's criticism did not serve feminist ends.

25. William Empson, "Virginia Woolf," appeared in *Scrutinies*, vol. 2, ed. Edgell Rickword (London: Wishart, 1931); its authors were asked to provide assessments of contemporary writers who have not yet been "rigged into an orthodoxy," as Rickword explained in the foreword to the volume (v). I quote the essay from *Argufying*, 443.

26. David Marno, *Death Be Not Proud: The Art of Holy Attention* (Chicago: University of Chicago Press, 2016).

27. Daniel Juan Gil, *Fate of the Flesh: Secularization and Resurrection in the Seventeenth Century* (New York: Fordham University Press, 2021).

28. Giulio J. Pertile, *Feeling Faint: Affect and Consciousness in the Renaissance* (Evanston, Ill.: Northwestern University Press, 2019).

1. Impersonal Eliot

1. All citations from "Tradition and the Individual Talent" are from T. S. Eliot, *Selected Essays* (London: Faber and Faber, 1951). I have also consulted and will refer to the annotated text in *The Complete Prose of T. S. Eliot: The Critical Edition*, ed. Anthony Cuda and Ronald Schuchard, available online through Project Muse, http://muse.jhu.edu/.

2. Richard Helpern describes Eliot's preposterous historical sense in *Shakespeare among the Moderns* (Ithaca: Cornell University Press, 1997), 3–4, as modernism's "historical allegory" of its dialectical relation to an early modernity at once remote and yet present.

3. For an analysis of "Tradition and the Individual Talent" that pursues its paradoxes, contradictions, reversals — its metaphorics, see Maud Ellmann, *The Poetics of Impersonality* (Cambridge, Mass.: Harvard University Press, 1987), 87ff.

4. All citations are from F. W. Bateson, "T.S. Eliot: "Impersonality" Fifty Years After," *Southern Review* 5, no. 3 (July 1969): 630–39.

5. More exact publication history than Bateson's can be found in the critical edition of Eliot's prose.

6. See Michael D. Snediker, *Queer Optimism: Lyric Personhood and Other Felicitous Persuasions* (Minneapolis: University of Minnesota Press, 2009), 230n80, for remarks about Bateson; see 39–40 on the *Inferno* encounter as one of queer poetic incitement. Contra Eliot, Snediker reads the sodomitical encounter against the injunction for the poet to suppress the personal. His argument is in line with the efforts of the contributors in Cassandra Laity and Nancy K. Kish, *Gender, Desire, and Sexuality in T. S. Eliot* (Cambridge: Cambridge University Press, 2004), to get past condemnation of Eliot's misogyny and possible homosexuality to find more constructive critical approaches.

7. Crossing genders, Dante compares the vapor of the burning stream that provides the atmosphere of his encounter with Brunetto Latini to "a well-known hot sulphurous spring near Viterbo" located near the prostitute quarter of the town (John D. Sinclair, ed. and trans., *The Divine Comedy of Dante Alighieri: Inferno* [New York: Oxford University Press, 1959], 188n4. All citations from this edition).

8. Bruce W. Holsinger, in "Sodomy and Resurrection: The Homoerotic Subject of the *Divine Comedy*," in Louise Fradenburg and Carla Freccero, eds., *Premodern Sexualities* (New York: Routledge, 1996), 249, hears "adora adora" in these lines; he also notes an allusion to Dido's words to Aeneas.

9. Leonard Barkan, *Transuming Passion: Ganymede and the Erotics of Humanism* (Stanford: Stanford University Press, 1991), 48–74, takes up the episode and its literary and

historical situation, including the sexual presumptions about
rhetorical pedagogy, as does Elizabeth Pittenger, "Explicit Ink,"
in Fradenburg and Freccero, *Premodern Sexualities*, 223–42;
Holsinger considers the broad ramifications of this topic.

10. See *The Poems of T. S. Eliot*, ed. Christopher Ricks and
Jim McCue (Baltimore: Johns Hopkins University Press, 2015),
1:1,014. I cite Eliot's poems from this edition.

11. All citations from John D. Sinclair, ed. and trans., *Dante's
Purgatorio* (New York: Oxford University Press, 1961). The
heightened affective language here matches the way Dante
speaks to Virgil, and Statius to Virgil, in the preceding cantos.

12. See Helen Gardner, *The Composition of Four Quartets*
(New York: Oxford University Press, 1978), as well as the
annotations to *Little Gidding* in *The Poems of T. S. Eliot*.
Dominic Menganiello, *T. S. Eliot and Dante* (London:
Macmillan, 1989), notices the connection between the reference
to *Inferno* xv in "Tradition and the Individual Talent" and
Little Gidding; Sharon Cameron, in an exacting reading of this
passage in *Little Gidding* in *Impersonality* (Chicago: University
of Chicago Press, 2007), 154–65, is one of the few critics to credit
Eliot's inspiration in Dante.

13. I cite "To Criticize the Critic," from T. S. Eliot, *To
Criticize the Critic and Other Writings* (Lincoln: University of
Nebraska Press, 1965). "What Dante Means to Me," is cited later
from this collection.

14. See, e.g., L. G. Salinger, *"The Revenger's Tragedy* and
the Morality Tradition," *Scrutiny* 6 (1937–8): 402–22, and
F. R. Leavis, "Imagery and Movement," *Scrutiny* 13 (1945):
119–34, both of which discuss Eliot's reading in "Tradition and
the Individual Talent." R. A. Foakes cites both in his Revels
edition (London: Methuen, 1966), noting that 3.2.75–98, the
lines Eliot cites are, thanks to him, "the most celebrated lines
in the play"; MacDonald P. Jackson, in Thomas Middleton,
The Collected Works, ed. Gary Taylor and John Lavagonino
(Oxford: Clarendon, 2007), i:572, follows suit in his gloss to the
same lines.

15. *Eingeschachelt* is translated "enclosed by, nestled within" in the critical edition; it proposes that Eliot may have taken the term from Adolf Stöhr's *Lehrbuch der Logik*, where it means, "how certain concepts are contained within related ones" (2:258n19).

16. I quote from Frank Kermode's introduction to *Selected Prose of T. S. Eliot* (San Diego: Harcourt, 1975), 13.

17. Eliot clings to his first impression even as he transmutes it. Perhaps he follows the prescription of Remy de Goncourt quoted as the epigraph to "The Perfect Critic": "Eriger en lois ses impressions personelles, c'est le grand effort d'un homme s'il est sincère"; T. S. Eliot, *The Sacred Wood* (Mineola, N.Y.: Dover, 1998), 1, from *Lettres à L'Amazone*, translated in the critical edition of Eliot's prose as "To erect his personal impressions into laws is the great effort of a man if he is sincere" (2:270n2). This citation might be put beside another from the same source, this one in Eliot's essay on Massinger: "La vie est un dépouillement. Le but de l'activité propre de l'homme est de nettoyer sa personalité" (217). This citation from *Le Problème du Style* is translated in the critical edition of Eliot's prose: "Life is a process of stripping down. The end of man's own activity is to clean his personality" (2:259n35).

18. Lawrence Ross notes how "for" is put to work to express both substitution and activity for the sake of someone else in his gloss on these lines in his Regents Renaissance Drama edition of *The Revenger's Tragedy* (Lincoln: University of Nebraska Press, 1966).

19. Martin Moraw, *"The Revenger's Trauerspiel*: Walter Benjamin and the Secularization of Theatricality," in Brian Walsh, ed., *The Revenger's Tragedy: A Critical Reader* (London: Bloomsbury, 2016), 166–87. I cite Walter Benjamin, *The Origin of German Tragic Drama*, trans. John Osborne (London: Verso, 1998), 166.

20. *"The Revenger's Tragedy* without Middleton," in Walsh, *The Revenger's Tragedy*, 101–22.

21. I cite "The Three Voices of Poetry," from T. S. Eliot, *On Poetry and Poets* (London: Faber and Faber, 1957), 98, 100, and

the Norton lecture from Eliot's *The Use of Poetry and the Use of Criticism* (Cambridge, Mass.: Harvard University Press, 1953), 137–38.

22. Stan Smith, "Paper Frontiers: Transgression and the Individual Talent," in Giovanni Cianci and Jason Harding, eds., *T. S. Eliot and the Concept of Tradition* (Cambridge: Cambridge University Press, 2007), 28.

23. I am grateful to Lara Bovilsky for helping me parse this sentence.

24. Aristotle, *De Anima*, trans. Hugh Lawson-Tancred (London: Penguin, 1986), 146; *De Anima*, trans. Mark Shiffman (Newburyport, Mass.: Focus, 2011), 41; *On the Soul*, trans. Joe Sachs (Santa Fe: Green Lion, 2004), 68; *On the Soul*, trans. W. S. Hett (Cambridge, Mass.: Harvard University Press, 1935), 49; Aristotle, *On the Soul*, trans. Fred D. Miller Jr. (Oxford: Oxford University Press, 2018), 14. The note is found on page 178, and the crux about human and cosmic mind is discussed in the introduction, xlii.

25. I cite Eliot's essay as published in appendix I to his dissertation, *Knowledge and Experience in the Philosophy of F. H. Bradley* (London: Faber and Faber, 1964), 183–84.

26. I will be citing from Giorgio Agamben, *Potentialities*, trans. Daniel Heller-Roazen (Stanford: Stanford University Press, 1999), the 1986 essay "On Potentiality," 177–84, as well as from other essays grouped under the subtitle "Potentiality": the 1988 "The Passion of Facticity," 85–204, and the 1990 *"Pardes*: The Writing of Potentiality," 205–19. The section ends with a 1996 essay contextualizing the meaning of life in Deleuze, "Absolute Immanence," 220–39.

27. Aristotle, *De Anima*, trans. Mark Shiffman, 102.

28. The essay is included in Giorgio Agamben's *The Fire and the Tale*, trans. Lorenzo Chiesa (Stanford: Stanford University Press, 2007), 33–56, from which I cite.

29. I cite from T. S. Eliot, *The Varieties of Metaphysical Poetry*, ed. Ronald Schuchard (San Diego: Harvest, 1993), 50.

30. Giorgio Agamben, *Stanzas: Word and Phantasm in*

Western Culture, trans. Ronald L. Martinez (Minneapolis: University of Minnesota Press, 1993), 84–85.

31. Ferdinand de Saussure, *Course in General Linguistics*, trans. Wade Baskin (New York: Philosophical Library, 1959), 120.

32. Frank Kermode, "Dissociation of Sensibility," *Kenyon Review* 19, no. 2 (Spring 1957): 169–94, traces the notion as it appears in Eliot's criticism and connects it to the revival of Donne initiated by Alexander Grosart's 1872 edition of Donne's poems and its coincidence with imagist poetry.

33. Citations in my text are from Giorgio Agamben, *What Is Philosophy?*, trans. Lorenzo Chiesa (Stanford: Stanford University Press, 2018).

34. T. S. Eliot, *For Lancelot Andrewes* (London: Faber & Gwyer, 1928), ix.

35. The Clark Lectures have been gathered along with the Turnbull Lectures derived from them, given at the Johns Hopkins University in 1933, and amply annotated by Ronald Schuchard, in *The Varieties of Metaphysical Poetry*.

36. T. S. Eliot, "Donne in Our Time," in *A Garland for John Donne*, ed. Theodore Spencer (Cambridge, Mass.: Harvard University Press, 1931), 1–19.

37. F. R. Leavis, *Revaluation: Tradition & Development in English Poetry* (London: Chatto & Windus, 1936), 10.

38. This is a point made in Joseph North, *Literary History: A Concise Political History* (Cambridge, Mass.: Harvard University Press, 2017), as I discuss in the Introduction.

39. T. S. Eliot, *George Herbert* (London: Longmans, Green, 1962).

2. Anonymous Woolf

1. I quote Virginia Woolf, *A Room of One's Own*, ed. Susan Gubar (Orlando: Harcourt, 2005).

2. Essays like "Tradition and the Female Talent," in *The War of the Words* (New Haven: Yale University Press, 1988), vol. 1 of Sandra Gilbert and Susan Gubar's *No Man's Land*

(New Haven: Yale University Press, 1994), and Florence Howe's edited collection, *Traditions and the Talents of Women* (Urbana: University of Illinois Press, 1991), including her own contribution to it, "T. S. Eliot, Virginia Woolf, and the Future of Tradition," initiated readings of Woolf addressing a tradition of women's writing ignored by T. S. Eliot.

3. Woolf has been faulted for claiming an absolute absence of women writers, e.g., by Margaret J. M. Ezell, "The Myth of Judith Shakespeare: Creating the Canon of Women's Literature," *NLH* 21, no. 3 (Spring 1990): 579–91; her subject is the existence of women writers free of the socioeconomic trammels of gender that impede free intellectual existence.

4. As Theodore Leinwand discusses in his chapter on Woolf in *The Great William: Writers Reading Shakespeare* (Chicago: University of Chicago Press, 2016), 67–71, Woolf's Judith Shakespeare figures her relation to her brother Thoby, whom she survived, and to whom she was attached by way of his attachment to Shakespeare (a feature also of the central character in *Jacob's Room*).

5. I cite Greene from E. K. Chambers, *William Shakespeare: A Study of Facts and Problems* (Oxford: Clarendon, 1930), 2:188.

6. I cite from *The Common Reader*, ed. Andrew McNeillie (Orlando: Harcourt, 1984) and *The Second Common Reader*, ed. McNeillie (San Diego: Harcourt, 1986). McNeillie's notes to *The Common Reader* in *The Essays of Virginia Woolf* (Orlando: Harcourt, 1994), 4:17–242, are expanded, expansive annotations, as are those for *The Common Reader: Second Series*, in *The Essays of Virginia Woolf*, ed. Stuart N. Clarke (London: Hogarth, 2009), 5:331–584.

7. Samuel Johnson, *Lives of the Poets* (London: Oxford University Press, 1952), 2:459.

8. "The Perfect Language," *TLS* 31 (May 1917), a review of the Loeb edition of *The Greek Anthology* (reprinted in *The Essays of Virginia Woolf*, ed. Andrew McNeillie [San Diego: Harcourt Brace Jovanovich, 1987], 2:114–22), offers an earlier take on the subject.

9. In her diary on December 8, 1929, Woolf recalls her father giving her Hakluyt: "It was the Elizabethan prose writers I loved first and most wildly, stirred by Hakluyt," entranced by the text, set to dreaming by it, modeling her prose on it (*The Diary of Virginia Woolf*, ed. Anne Olivier Bell [San Diego: Harcourt Brace, 1980], 3:273). "Trafficks and Discoveries," *Speaker* (August 12, 1906), in *The Essays of Virginia Woolf*, ed. Andrew McNeillie (San Diego: Harcourt Brace Jovanovich, 1986), 1:120–24, reviews a 1906 edition of Hakluyt and anticipates the *Common Reader* essay in describing the pleasure she took from its words and objects: "a fragrance seems to rise from the page itself" (122). "Trafficks and Discoveries," *TLS* (December 12, 1918), in *The Essays of Virginia Woolf* (San Diego: Harcourt Brace Jovanovich, 1987), 2:329–36, also emphasizes the affordances of Hakluyt and provides some referents for episodes also recalled in *The Common Reader*. "Reading," in *The Essays of Virginia Woolf* (San Diego: Harcourt Brace Jovanovich, 1988), 3:141–61, published posthumously in *The Captain's Death Bed* (1950), recalls the 1918 essay on Hakluyt and anticipates discussions of Sir Thomas Browne as well, as does "Sir Thomas Browne," *The Essays of Virginia Woolf*, 3:368–72.

10. Woolf had written on Cavendish as early as a 1911 review of a joint biography, "The Duke and Duchess of Newcastle-upon-Tyne," in *The Essays of Virginia Woolf*, 1:345–51; some citations and phrases from this piece reappear in the 1925 essay.

11. Woolf leveled a similar charge against what neoclassical dramatists had made of Greek tragedy, its heroines who are not characters, but abstractions (Voltaire and Addison are her examples): "the greatest bores and the most demoralising companions in the world" (27).

12. Woolf records her writing of these essays in volume 4 of *The Diary of Virginia Woolf*, ed. Anne Olivier Bell (San Diego: Harcourt Brace, 1983). Her interest in Donne was longstanding, as can be seen in a May 21, 1912, letter to Lytton Strachey about her discussion with Desmond MacCarthy about his plans to write about Donne; see volume 1 of *The Letters of Virginia Woolf*, ed.

Nigel Nicolson and Joanne Trautmann (San Diego: Harcourt
Brace, 1975), 498. Sally Greene, "Entering Woolf's Renaissance
Imaginary: A Second Look at *The Second Common Reader*,"
in Beth Carole Rosenberg and Jeanne Dubino, eds., *Virginia
Woolf and the Essay* (New York: St. Martin's, 1997), 81–95,
emphasizes the pertinence of the Renaissance to Woolf's agenda
for contemporary literature.

13. The erotic figuration of the relations between Harvey and
Spenser, between Spenser, Sidney, and his sister, are my topic in
Jonathan Goldberg, *Sodometries* (Stanford: Stanford University
Press, 1992), chap. 3, "Spenser's Familiar Letters," 63–101.

14. On this topic, see Juliet Fleming, *Graffiti and the Writing
Arts of Early Modern England* (Philadelphia: University of
Pennsylvania Press, 2001), 46ff.

15. In discussing this project, I depend upon Brenda R.
Silver, "'Anon' and 'The Reader': Virginia Woolf's Last Essays,"
Twentieth-Century Literature 25, no. 3–4 (Autumn–Winter 1979):
356–441.

16. *The Diary of Virginia Woolf*, ed. Anne Olivier Bell (San
Diego: Harcourt Brace, 1984), 5:318.

17. Virginia Woolf, *The Death of the Moth and Other Essays*
(Harmondsworth: Penguin, 1961), 173.

18. Gilles Deleuze, "Literature and Life," trans. Daniel W.
Smith and Michael Greco, *Critical Inquiry* 23, no. 2 (Winter
1997): 225–30. I depend upon Derek Ryan, who concludes
*Virginia Woolf and the Materiality of Theory: Sex, Animal,
Life* (Edinburgh: Edinburgh University Press, 2013), 197, by
mentioning this text as the conclusion to his Deleuzian reading
of Woolf that looks at natural objects, animals, and gender fluidity
to explore the materiality of life in a range of her texts. See
Deleuze, *Pure Immanence: Essays on a Life*, trans. Anne Boyman
(New York: Zone, 2001), where he describes "a life" as manifest
"when the life of the individual gives way to an impersonal
and yet singular life that releases a pure event freed from the
accidents of internal and external life" (28).

19. I cite "The Faery Queen," from *The Essays of Virginia Woolf*, vol. 6, ed. Stuart N. Clarke (London: Hogarth, 2011).

20. "A Sketch of the Past" is included in *Moments of Being*, ed. Jeanne Schulkind (San Diego: Harcourt Brace, 1985, 1976), 67.

21. *The Diary of Virginia Woolf*, ed. Anne Olivier Bell (San Diego: Harcourt Brace, 1980), 3:300–301.

3. Ambiguous Empson

1. William Empson, *Seven Types of Ambiguity* (New York: New Directions, 1947, 1966), ix. All citations in my text are from this edition. James Smith's review, "Books of the Quarter," first appeared in *The Criterion* 10, no. 41 (July 1931): 739–42, and is reprinted in John Constable, ed., *Critical Essays on William Empson* (Aldershot: Scolar, 1993), 42–45, from which I quote.

2. See William Empson, *Some Versions of Pastoral* (London: Chatto & Windus, 1950), 80, for Empson's mention of James Smith, "On Metaphysical Poetry," *Scrutiny* 2, no. 3 (December 1933): 222–39.

3. Helen Thaventhiran, *Radical Empiricists: Five Modernist Close Readers* (Oxford: Oxford University Press, 2015). She does this in the first of her two chapters distinguishing Empson from the later new critics (chap. 3, "Emendation: William Empson and the Textual Crux"), following it with another on his embrace of the heresy of paraphrase (chap. 4, "Paraphrase: William Empson's Cheerful Heresies"), 92–122.

4. Marshall Brown finds this also to be the case in "Reading Empson: *The Structure of Complex Words*," *ELH* 88, no. 3 (Fall 2021):743–64, esp. 750–53.

5. The eight-line poem can be found in its entirety in Arthur Waley, *A Hundred and Seventy Chinese Poems* (London: Chiswick, 1918), where it is titled "New Corn," and appears in the selection of poems by the fourth-century poet T'ao Ch'ien (chap. 3, no. 12). Eugene Euyang, "T'ao Ch'ien's 'The

Seasons Come and Go: Four Poems' — A Meditation," *Chinese Literature: Essays, Articles, Reviews* 20 (December 1998): 1–9, notes that Waley's "swiftly" and "stillness" are not literally in the Chinese, but that the words are not amiss, nor, he comments, are Empson's observations about them as keys to the temporalities in the poem.

6. Irad Kimhi, *Thinking and Being* (Cambridge, Mass.: Harvard University Press, 2018), argues this monist point from the perspective of a philosophical logic shaped by Wittgenstein and inspired by reading of a fragment of Parmenides' poem *On Nature* and the metaphysics of Aristotle and Plato.

7. Michael Wood, *On Empson* (Princeton: Princeton University Press, 2017), 1.

8. Paul de Man's essay first appeared as "Impasse de la critique formaliste," *Critique* 14, no. 109 (June 1956): 483–500. I will be citing it in the English translation in De Man, *Blindness and Insight* (Minneapolis: University of Minnesota Press, 1983).

9. Cf. Barbara Johnson's brilliant reading of the relation of "leaves" and "leave" in sonnet 73, in "Speech Therapy," in *Shakesqueer*, ed. Madhavi Menon (Durham, N.C.: Duke University Press, 2011), 328–32. Stephen Booth attests to his inspiration for his edition of Shakespeare's sonnets (which lists all possible meanings) in Empson's demonstration of the inextricability of "lines" and "life" in sonnet 16, yet another directed at W. H. in *Shakespeare's Sonnets* (New Haven: Yale University Press, 1977), xiii.

10. Empson's reading of "A Valediction: Of Weeping" continued to be on his mind for many years; he revisits it, for example, in his 1957 essay "Donne the Spaceman"; see Empson, *Essays on Renaissance Literature*, ed. John Haffenden (Cambridge: Cambridge University Press, 1993), 1:106ff. Haffenden's introduction to the volume does a very thorough job of explicating Empson's main concerns from 1949 on.

11. Empson recoiled at Eliot's claim in "Donne in Our Time" that Donne "was no . . . sceptic" (*A Garland for John Donne*, ed. Theodore Spencer [Cambridge, Mass.: Harvard University Press,

1931], 11–12), in "Donne in the New Edition," in Empson, *Essays on Renaissance Literature*, 1:130.

12. The best guide to this subject is Aaron Kunin, *Love Three* (Seattle: Wave, 2019).

13. In "More Lurid Figures: De Man Reading Empson," in Christopher Norris and Nigel Mapp, eds., *William Empson: The Critical Achievement* (Cambridge: Cambridge University Press, 1993), 213–42, Neil Hertz takes up these gendered complications to de Man's reading.

14. A convenient summary of his argument with Tuve is offered by John Haffenden, ed., in William Empson, *The Strengths of Shakespeare's Shrew* (Sheffield: Sheffield Academic Press, 1996), 119–28.

15. Rosemond Tuve, *A Reading of George Herbert* (Chicago: University of Chicago Press, 1952), 63.

16. Empson, *The Strengths of Shakespeare's Shrew*, 124. "Rosemond Tuve does not differ from me as much as she supposes," he notes.

17. Originally published in 1927; I cite from the first volume of the second edition of *The Poems and Letters of Andrew Marvell* (Oxford: Clarendon, 1952).

18. Here I part company with Ryan Netzley's rich and provocative "Sameness and the Poetics of Nonrelation: Andrew Marvell's 'The Garden,'" *PMLA* 132, no. 3 (2017): 580–94, which does not engage the complexity that Empson explores.

19. Bradbrook presumably conveyed this thought to Empson privately; it is not found in "The Criticism of William Empson," *Scrutiny* 2/3 (December 1933): 253–77, which closes with a brief discussion of Empson's essay on "The Garden," but not to make this point. In his note to Empson's mention of Bradbrook in *Some Versions of Pastoral* (Oxford: Oxford University Press, 2020), 87, Seamus Perry, editor of this newly annotated text, refers the reader to his introduction, xxiii, where he cites Bradbrook's *Scrutiny* essay to gloss Empson's mention of her.

20. This is where Empson concluded the earlier versions of his essay that appeared in *Studies in English Literature* 13, no. 3

(August 1932): 163–68, and in *Scrutiny* 1, no. 3 (December 1932): 236–40. His brief essay stays close to the passages inspired by stanza vi that have guided my analysis thus far.

21. See "Part II. Shakespeare and the Spirits," in William Empson, *Essays on Renaissance Literature*, ed. John Haffenden (Cambridge: Cambridge University Press, 1994), 2:155–248.

22. Empson refers here to I. A. Richards, "Human Nature: An Early Chinese Argument," *Psyche* 47 (January 1932): 62–77. The essay lies behind passages in the opening chapters in *Mencius on the Mind* (London: Kegan Paul, 1932), 23–26, 44–60. Richards modified somewhat the division between West and East that seems to shape his argument there; in "Mencius Through the Looking-Glass" (in *So Much Nearer* [New York: Harcourt, Brace & World, 1960, 1968]), he elevates the thought of Mencius against the pretenses of science as offering "one of the most satisfying modes of human living that have been tried" (215), though he remained committed to Basic English as a kind of universal medium for cross-cultural communication. Richards turned to Confucius in *Practical Criticism* (New York: Harcourt, Brace, 1929) in the chapter on "Doctrine in Poetry" occasioned by readers who couldn't appreciate Donne's sonnet "At the round earth's imagined corners blow" because of its vision of the Last Judgment: Empson's position about "What if this present were the world's last night," in *Seven Types of Ambiguity* (145–46). Here he offers the possibility that readerly sincerity could be awakened against prejudicial antipathy, defining it as Confucius does in *Chung Yung* as "obedience to that tendency which 'seeks' a more perfect order in the mind" (288) faced with human loneliness, our mortality in an infinite, unknowable universe. See David Marno, *Death Be Not Proud* (Chicago: University of Chicago Press, 2016) for the aptness of Richards to Donne, although not in the terms of the relation between Richards and Empson acknowledged at the opening of Empson's discussion of "The Garden."

23. See *The Face of the Buddha*, ed. Rupert Arrowsmith (Oxford: Oxford University Press, 2016), 110, where Empson

cites from 1:222 of Charles Eliot's three-volume *Hinduism and Buddhism* (London: Routledge & Kegan Paul, 1921); there Eliot concludes a discussion of the eightfold path that began on page 213.

24. Thanissaro Bhikkhu, *Handful of Leaves* (Redwood City, Calif.: Sati Center for Buddhist Studies, 2003), 2:274.

25. William Empson, "The Faces of Buddha," *Listener* (February 5, 1936), reprinted in *Argufying* (Iowa City: University of Iowa Press, 1987), 573. This sentence also appears at the opening of *The Face of the Buddha*, 5.

Index

Jonathan Goldberg is Arts and Sciences Distinguished Professor Emeritus at Emory University. His many books include *Come As You Are, After Eve Kosofsky Sedgwick*; *Saint Marks: Words, Images, and What Persists*; *Melodrama: An Aesthetics of Impossibility*; and *Sodometries: Renaissance Texts, Modern Sexualities*. His writing centers on early modernity but ranges from Sappho and Willa Cather to Patricia Highsmith and Todd Haynes in exploring questions of materiality and sexuality.